THAI
VEGETARIAN COOKING

THAI
VEGETARIAN COOKING

VATCHARIN BHUMICHITR

PAVILION

For my Aunt Chindar, who taught me to love good food.

First published in Great Britain in 1991 by
Pavilion Books Limited
26, Upper Ground, London SE1 9PD

Text copyright © Vatcharin Bhurnichitr 1991
Photographs copyright © John Ferro Sims 1991
Photograph on p.96 copyright © Tourist Authority of Thailand

Designed by Lisa Tai

A CIP catalogue record for this book is available from the British Library
ISBN 1 85145 891 3

Printed and bound in Singapore by Kyodo

10 9 8 7 6 5 4

CONTENTS

INTRODUCTION

I was not a vegetarian when I began this book, nor am I one now that it is finished – but a lot has happened in between. At the outset I imagined that I would simply search out Thai vegetarians and gather together their favourite recipes. It was not to prove so easy. As soon as I began, I discovered that there is nothing straightforward about vegetarianism in Thailand.

First there is the question of religion. Surely, I am often asked, as a Buddhist you must be opposed to killing animals for food, for didn't the Buddha forbid it? Well, he certainly forbade monks to take life, including animal life, but some argue that monks are not forbidden to eat meat when it is given to them during their alms gathering. Indeed they are ordered not to refuse whatever they are given, which means in effect that they must eat meat. That is the official Thai Buddhist line. And yet Thais undoubtedly share an aversion to killing animals. Many believe it is somehow more sinful to kill a large animal than a small one, though this may be due to the Hindu missionaries who once came to Thailand and whose beliefs can still be traced in many village superstitions. As a result, few Thais choose to

(From left to right) Baskets of kaffir lime leaves, galangal and lemon grass in Bangkok's central market

6

become butchers and the job is usually left to immigrant workers – Pathans for beef, Chinese for pork.

It was not hard to find Thais who prefer meat-free meals, but they usually simply drop meat or fish from a recipe while continuing to use flavourings such as fish sauce. Obviously this is just tinkering with ordinary Thai dishes and does not constitute a true vegetarian cuisine. Indeed attitudes to meat-eating vary widely across the country. I was told that the Isaan men in the northeast occasionally eat raw meat at special festivities as a sign of virility, but that the people of central Thailand find even rare meat or any sign of blood in food totally unacceptable. Throughout the country women, children and the aged appear to have a more vegetable-orientated diet, though probably for economic rather than health reasons. How different it all seemed from China, where Buddhist monks are totally vegetarian and where there is an entire vegetarian culture and cuisine parallel to the meat-eating world. Then, just when I thought there was no point in going on with this book, a revelation occurred which showed me that I had been looking in completely the wrong direction.

While on a visit to Thailand my brother took me to the Weekend Market in Bangkok where he had heard there was a vegetarian pavilion much frequented by devotees. I went without much hope, expecting to find the usual array of stir-fry vegetables with the meat left out. Instead I found that whole 'other' cuisine I had been looking for. It was a revelation in the use of raw materials to create not facsimiles of meat dishes as so often happens in vegetarian cookery, but something quite new and different. I ate things that day that were not like anything I had previously come across in Thai food.

I had been looking to the past, trying to find a tradition that did not exist. There is no ancient vegetarian culture; instead I was witnessing the beginnings of a new one. Vegetarianism is catching on fast. Friends

with restaurants have told me how in response to increasing demand they are experimenting with vegetarian dishes, sometimes drawing on Chinese examples, but just as often looking into the heart of Thai cooking to find new responses. While still in Bangkok, I was advised to go to the Whole Earth restaurant, the only true vegetarian place outside the Weekend Market. I ate there, and was won over. I quickly began assembling recipes from contacts in Bangkok, but now I knew that I was going to have to join this creative experiment myself.

Back in London I was suddenly presented with a glorious opportunity. My cousin decided to open a restaurant in Bethnal Green and asked me to help. I persuaded her to open the first Thai vegetarian restaurant in Britain, which we baptised the Thai Garden. I then set about creating the menu, training the chef and generally exercising my knowledge and imagination. This book is the result. It is in every sense original, and is arguably the first book on Thai vegetarian cooking. Writing it has certainly changed me for while I still occasionally eat meat and am not a vegetarian by conviction, I more often find myself turning to the recipes here, simply because I find them more enjoyable than ordinary Thai food. And that is something I would never have predicted when I began.

NOTE: Most Western cooks will probably be used to grinding or blending ingredients in a food processor, however, a mortar and pestle, while appearing more arduous, will give the sort of texture required for Thai food. For very fine grinding of spices you could use a coffee-grinder but you will need to keep one especially for this as the pungent flavours can never be completely removed.

Woman pounding brown rice to separate the husk

EQUIPMENT

Apart from equipment normally available in any reasonably set up Western kitchen you will need a mortar and pestle and a steamer. While not absolutely essential a wok, an electric rice steamer, and a heavy chopping 'axe' will prove useful if you plan to cook oriental food frequently.

WEIGHTS AND MEASURES

Unless otherwise stated, each recipe is seen as being part of a meal for two or three people in which at least three other dishes would be served. Portions are quite small and aside from the section on One Dish Meals you should always plan to make a balanced meal of several dishes, say two from the Main Dishes chapter along with a curry and a soup – plus rice of course!

Dry measures Small amounts are measured in teaspoons and tablespoons. There is no appreciable difference between the UK and US versions. Larger amounts are given in imperial measures with a metric equivalent. UK and US dry measures are the same.

Liquid measures UK and US liquid measures *are* different. In this book liquid measures are set out as follows: first in imperial, second in the metric equivalent and third in US cups, thus: 8fl oz/240ml/1 cup.

TECHNIQUE

Very few of the recipes in this book give any indication of cooking times. This is because most oriental cooking is based on the 'stir-fry' technique where everything happens at great speed. To attempt a breakdown of the component times in such a procedure would be meaningless. The basic rule for Thai cooking is that all ingredients should be ready before cooking begins – this usually means that each item has been cut small enough to cook quickly. These ingredients are then 'tossed' into a frying pan/skillet or wok, stirred very briefly and turned on to a serving dish at once. If anything has to be set aside it will not need to be kept warm as it will be used almost immediately.

The arduous part of Thai cooking is getting everything ready, the actual cooking is over in minutes, which makes it a delight for the party-giver. I do understand, however, that many Westerners have a built-in resistance to this sort of technique and worry about whether things are adequately cooked, so it is essential to realize that all ingredients will be *al dente* or 'firm to the teeth' and that you cannot be too quick as the ingredients will go on cooking for a short time after they are turned on to the serving dish. The best advice I can give is: 'Don't worry, just do it.' If you have the chance to watch an oriental chef at work you will be astonished at the speed. To repeat: when a recipe says: 'Add all the ingredients, stirring constantly', you should put each ingredient in turn into the wok, stir once, add the next, stir once, and so on and after the final stir for the last ingredient *you have finished*. The trick is that the ingredients are graded from hard to soft so that those with more solid stems or a firmer texture are in the wok just a little bit longer. Highly skilled oriental chefs work at high speed on a high flame, lifting away the wok to vary the temperature. The beginner should choose a medium high heat which will mean less urgency and less risk of burning or over-cooking.

INGREDIENTS

None of the recipes in this book features any product from an abattoir or butcher's shop, nor is fish sauce used as a condiment. I have used eggs and to alert Vegan readers the symbol Ⓔ indicates where this is so.

Here is a selection of the more commonly used ingredients; some are more fully described later in the book, as shown.

(From left to right) Coconut milk, chili sauce, dark soy sauce, yellow bean sauce, light soy sauce, white vinegar

Aubergine/Eggplant See p. 56.

Bandan leaf (also pandanus or screwpine) The leaves of a scented flower, which are used to add a fresh smell and flavour to oriental sweets. It is usual to buy the entire cut plant with approximately 10 long thin leaves.

Basil, holy and sweet Fresh holy basil can be bought in oriental stores and is also available dried. It has a darker leaf than the European sweet basil, a common substitute, and a slightly aniseed, sharper flavour.

Banana leaf This large ribbed leaf has many uses in the East from roofing to cooking, where its function is that of the vine leaf in Mediterranean food. When used as a wrapping during steaming the leaf imparts a vague flavour of fine tea. Alternatively, foil can be used, but of course no flavour will result.

Beancurd (tofu) See p. 91.

Bean sauce Black bean, yellow bean and red bean sauces are equally salty and flavourful, and interchangeable: choice often depends on what would look more attractive in the dish. All are made from preserved soy beans and are usually available in bottles or jars.

Bitter melon Pear shaped, with green warty skin, this is an immature melon sometimes compared to cucumbers that have the bitterness of chicory leaves. Can be found in most Chinese supermarkets.

Cabbage Three varieties of cabbage are used in this book: the red and white cabbages common in the West, which are often used for salad dishes, and the Chinese cabbage sometimes known as Chinese leaves or Peking cabbage, now available in ordinary supermarkets as well as oriental stores.

Chilis See p. 32.

Coconut milk I have assumed that you will use tinned coconut milk. If the recipe requires coconut cream, open the tin without shaking and separate the thicker white fluid from the remaining transparent liquid.

Coriander (Chinese parsley, cilantro) Coriander is used extensively as a flavouring, and as a garnish. The root is also used, often pounded with garlic and other ingredients to make a marinade. Leaf and root are bought complete. In the West the roots are often cut short and so must be used with an inch or so of the leaf stalk. After rinsing and drying, the roots will keep in a

Krachai

sealed container in a refrigerator for several days. Coriander is now readily available in supermarkets and stores as well as in specialist shops.

The seeds, readily available, are used in curry pastes.

Curry, paste and powder Several kinds of paste are used in Thai cuisine and most are available ready-made in foil packets. But it is much more satisfactory to make your own (p. 105). When curry powder is stipulated in a recipe a ready-made mild Indian curry powder can be used.

Galangal (galanga, galangale, kha, laos) This looks similar to ginger root, but has a more translucent skin and a pinkish tinge. It is peeled like ginger, but sliced rather than slivered. It is available fresh in oriental stores and can also be bought dried.

Garlic Indispensable in Thai cooking. The Asian variety is much smaller than that usual in Europe and the recipes have assumed the use of the European type. While many people use garlic crushers, I much prefer to chop the cloves finely by hand. Pickled garlic can be bought in jars from Asian food stores.

Ginger Always used in fresh root form and widely available. The root is first peeled and usually sliced thin, slivered, or diced very small.

Kaffir Lime This is roughly the same size and shape as the common lime but with a knobbly skin. The skin is often used, chopped, in recipes for curry paste. The skin of the common lime may be substituted.

Krachai Also known as lesser ginger, it is of the same family as ginger and galangal, though a smaller root. It has a fiercer, wilder flavour than ginger. Sometimes available fresh in oriental stores. It can also be found dried in small packets and in this form should be soaked in water for 30 minutes before use.

Lemon grass An indispensable ingredient in Thai cuisine. The stalks are bought in bundles of 6-8 and are usually 7–8 inches/18–20cm long. The ends are trimmed and the stalk finely sliced. One average stalk will give approximately 3tbsp/45ml finely sliced lemon grass. The stalks will last quite well for 2–3 weeks in a refrigerator, and chopped lemon grass can be put in a plastic bag and frozen. Dried chopped lemon grass in small packets is also available.

Lime leaves These are the dark green glossy leaves of the kaffir lime and impart a pungent lemon-lime flavour. They are available in some oriental stores and are worth looking for – they are usually packaged as small branches in a plastic bag. They keep well and can be frozen. They are also available dried. Slicing is best achieved by using kitchen scissors to cut fine strips of the leaf.

Long bean 1–3 feet (up to 1 metre) long, the aptly named long bean resembles an overgrown stringbean, although it is of a different genus. However, because the taste is similar, the easier-to-find string bean can be used as a substitute, though the long bean has a crunchier texture and cooks faster. Choose darker rather than lighter coloured beans, preferably with smaller bean seeds inside the pods.

Moong beans (mung or green gram) Small dried yellow beans available from oriental stores. The soaking time varies depending on the recipe.

Morning glory (water spinach) This vegetable has long jointed stems which remain firm when cooked, in contrast to the arrow-shaped leaves, which go limp. The flavour is slightly of spinach. The leaves quickly turn yellow and go bad.

Mushrooms See p. 45.

Long bean

Oil Almost any vegetable oil will serve, except olive oil, which imparts a flavour quite foreign to Thai dishes. Normally I prefer to use groundnut, peanut, soy, safflower or sunflower oils. Most Thai recipes begin by frying garlic in the oil to flavour it.

Papaya (pawpaw) A large green gourd-like fruit with soft yellow-orange flesh. When unripe and still green the flesh is used as a vegetable.

Preserved turnip (chi po) Used finely chopped and in small amounts and found in Oriental stores.

Preserved radish (tang chi) This is often found whole or in slices, in vacuum-sealed packages from Chinese or oriental stores. We use it in small amounts, slivered or chopped, to add texture and flavour.

Rice See p. 19.

Sago (Sa ku) A starch made from the pith of the sago palm. When boiled the hard semi-transparent whitish grains expand into little balls of sweet transparent jelly.

Soy sauce I have made a distinction between 'light' and 'dark' soy sauce, the dark being slightly thicker, sweeter, and usually a little more expensive. It is used as much to add a little colour to a dish as for flavour. Light and dark soy sauces are often used together.

Spring flower (also gui chi or flowering Chinese chives) Long thin leaves topped with small white bulbs. The whole plant is eaten and tastes slightly of garlic.

Sticky rice See p. 50.

Tamarind The pulp of the fruit is exported in a compressed packaged form. To extract the juice or water, the pulp should be dissolved in hot water and the resulting liquid strained. It is quite sour and if it is not available lemon juice may be substituted in twice the amount of tamarind required.

Taro This rather bland-tasting tuber is used as a vegetable or pulped to make a dessert with added flavourings.

Turmeric Another member of the ginger family, this can occasionally be found fresh in oriental stores, but is more frequently available in powdered form.

Vinegar Most white vinegars can be used, but I prefer the authenticity of the rice vinegar which is readily available in all Chinese and other Asian stores.

White Radish (Mooli) A root vegetable, originating in Asia but now common in the West, where it is often served as a salad vegetable. When cooked it loses its cool sharpness and resembles turnip.

Wingbean Like mangetout or snow peas the whole of this vegetable, both the casing and the tiny inner beans, is used. The greenest will be freshest.

THE THAI MEAL

Apart from a quick dish of noodles or fried rice eaten at speed during a busy day, no Thai would choose to eat alone. The ideal Thai meal consists of a number of small dishes shared by a group of friends. Rice is ladled on to each plate, all the dishes are put out at the same time and everyone dips a spoon into the bowl of his or her choice, carrying a little back to the plate to be eaten with the rice. The Thais use spoon and fork and not chopsticks (except for noodles) and no one scoops large quantities of food on to their plate – sharing is essential.

The perfect meal should contain a balance of sweet and sour, hot and cool, fried and steamed dishes. The following is a rough guide to that sort of balance in a meal suitable for four people.

First: one or two dishes of what I have described as 'Starters and Snacks' plus one yam dish, brought out before the main meal to be nibbled with drinks but essentially part of the full meal when it arrives.
Then: rice with one soup, one curry, and two main dishes.
Then: fruit and/or dessert.
Sample menus are offered at the end of the book.

Women at a village temple preparing red curry paste for a festival feast

ONE-DISH MEALS

THE RICE MOTHER

In a traditional country home, where the old ways are still respected, a little ceremony takes place before each meal. The father of the house takes a little rice, forms it into a ball with his fingers and places it outside on the land so that birds and insects may share the earth's bounty with his family.

It is a charming act but one that is also deeply significant. You have only to travel a short distance from the mad bustle of Bangkok to see with your own eyes the importance of rice to my people. In a way it is the key to everything. The very word for rice – *kow* – means not only the little white grain but food itself, while *od kow di*, literally 'without rice', signifies starvation. Far from the cities, peasant farmers still honour the ancient Rice Goddess, Mae Posop or Mother Posop, who they believe will bless or punish them according to the respect they show for her gifts. In the villages uneaten rice is never wasted, but always re-cooked in some way. The rice plant itself is treated with great care: the paddies are protected from animals and not a single grain is wasted once it has been harvested. The closeness of the farmer to his land is shown in the ceremonies that are associated with rice. When the

Paddy field near Petchaburi

17

plants start to seed the farmer will say that his rice 'becomes pregnant' and to please the Rice Mother he will take gifts of fruit to the field and will comb and perfume one of his rice plants as if dressing the hair of the Goddess herself. When the rice has been harvested and threshed a feast is prepared for Mae Posop, without meat or fish, an echo of the Hindu vegetarianism that is one of the strands making up the complex weave of Thai religious belief.

For the city dweller to go out to the countryside is a refreshing experience. One of my college friends is now the village schoolmaster in a small hamlet about twenty minutes from the town of Petchaburi, south west of Bangkok. To visit him is to enter a world we forget at our peril. The daily life of the farmers and their families is essentially simple, their usual food is rice, with vegetables, a little fried fish and a spicy sauce, but when temple feast days come round everyone gets together to produce a meal to remember.

Those who know Thai food only from visits to city restaurants, either in Thailand or in the West, probably have a false impression of the cooking of my native land. What such restaurants serve is a fairly recent hybrid of traditional country food merged with the more elaborate dishes once reserved for the royal and noble families of the capital. To someone thinking of cooking Thai food, the sight of those sumptuous meals made up of several different dishes, prettily decorated with carved vegetables, is understandably off-putting. But we are no different from anyone else in needing simple meals – whether for the farmer working out in his rice paddy or the city worker dashing from the office with only an hour to spare. Happily, if one goes back to the simple food of the countryside there is help to hand, for rice and noodles are the best possible bases for quick wholesome meals.

This first chapter sets out five rice and fourteen noodle dishes, each enough for one person. It provides a gentle introduction to the many techniques of Thai cooking. There are two slightly more complex recipes at the end of the chapter to prepare you for what follows. The joy of these first recipes for vegetarians is twofold. Firstly they can be 'thrown' together from easily available materials – the rice dishes, for example, are made with rice left over from an earlier meal. And secondly, they are quick to make; most of the time involved is in the preparation, and the cooking time is negligible.

My Western vegetarian friends, in the midst of a busy day when they do not want to spend much time cooking, too often find themselves reduced to cheese-based snacks, and I trust that this chapter will show that a viable alternative is easily to hand. I hope too that as you cook and eat your rice you can spare a thought for that distant farmer out in his field planting and harvesting the grain or offering his ball of rice to the Rice Mother in an act of kindness to all living things.

Kanom Jin, *fresh white noodles made on special occasions*

RICE

The first essential of any oriental meal is good rice. For the vegetarian, this has an added importance in that the vitamins and roughage found in the grains help ensure a truly balanced diet. Fortunately Thailand has some of the best rice in Asia, and indeed the export of our surplus harvests is a mainstay of the economy.

A Thai cook will know from experience whether rice is young or old; young rice needs to be cooked in less water than old, as it still contains some natural moisture. In Thailand we use what we call 'fragrant' rice, a good quality long-grain rice. But it is probable that all rice available in Europe and North America is 'old', and therefore completely dry and will need slightly more water to cook in.

An electric rice cooker is a wise investment for regular rice eaters, otherwise a little technique is needed to get your rice light and fluffy, with each grain separate.

1lb/450g/2 cups rice
1 pint/500ml/2 cups water

Rinse the rice thoroughly at least three times in cold water until the water runs clear. Put the rice in a heavy saucepan and add the water. Cover and quickly bring to the boil. Uncover, and while it is cooking stir vigorously until all the water has been absorbed by the rice. Turn the heat down as low as possible, re-cover (put a layer of foil under the lid if necessary to make sure of a tight fit) and gently heat for up to 20 minutes until the rice becomes dry and each grain is separate and light.

For sticky or glutinous rice see p. 50.

FRIED RICE WITH TURMERIC

KHAO PAD KAMIN

We Thais vary in skin colour from light brown to light yellow, though in the past the most beautiful shade was thought to be the golden hue of a statue of the Buddha. To achieve this impossible colouring it was not unknown for people to help nature by rubbing their skin with turmeric powder. Today turmeric is no longer used as a cosmetic, but this golden dish is a pleasant reminder of that peculiar bygone fashion.

2tbsp/30ml oil
1 garlic clove, finely chopped
2oz/60g/1 small onion, diced
2oz/60g/1 carrot, diced
1tsp/5ml turmeric powder
8oz/240g/2 cups cooked rice
$^1/_2$tsp/2.5ml sugar
3tsp/45ml light soy sauce
$^1/_2$tsp/2.5ml chili powder
2oz/60g/$^1/_2$cup ready-fried beancurd, quartered

To garnish
1 spring onion/scallion, finely chopped
1 medium tomato, cut into wedges
3inch/7.5cm piece cucumber, in $^1/_2$inch/2.5cm slices

In a wok or frying pan/skillet, heat the oil until a light haze appears. Add the garlic and fry until golden brown. Stirring all the time, add the onion, carrots, turmeric powder and cooked rice. Stir thoroughly. Add the sugar, light soy sauce and chili powder. Stir thoroughly. Add the beancurd, stir and turn on to a serving dish. Sprinkle with spring onion rings. Arrange the tomato and cucumber at the side of the dish.

Fried rice with basil (left), turmeric (front) and pineapple (back)

FRIED RICE WITH PINEAPPLE

KHAO PAD SUPPAROT

As this dish is served, rather dramatically, in the hollowed out pineapple itself, it is clearly destined to be party food. Only a small amount of the flesh of the fruit is needed for the rice so there is ample left for a dessert. I make no apologies for the fact that Thai people are always boasting about how their fruit is the sweetest in the world, because it is. Our pineapples are truly exceptional. Obviously you will have to make do with what your market can offer but take care to give the leaves a not-too-hard tug to make sure they come away easily, the best sign of ripeness. If the fruit is not so sweet it won't matter for the part used in this savoury dish but you will need to doctor the remainder if you plan to serve it as a dessert.

*1 large fresh pineapple, sliced lengthwise in half, the
flesh removed, and cut into cubes and set aside
1 slice wholewheat bread, diced, deep-fried
with 1oz/30g/$^1/_4$cup cashew nuts
until golden brown
2tbsp/30ml oil
1 garlic clove, finely chopped
2oz/60g/$^2/_3$cup pre-soaked dried black
fungus mushrooms, cut small
2oz/60g/1 small onion, diced
3oz/90g/$^2/_3$cup pineapple cubes
8oz/240g/2 cups cooked rice
3tbsp/45ml light soy sauce
$^1/_2$tsp/2.5ml sugar
$^1/_2$tsp/2.5ml ground white pepper*

*To garnish
1 spring onion/scallion, finely chopped into rings
coriander leaves*

In a wok or frying pan/skillet, heat the oil until a light haze appears. Add the garlic and fry until golden brown. Stirring all the time, add the mushrooms, onion, pineapple, rice, light soy sauce, sugar and pepper, and mix thoroughly. Add the fried bread and cashew nuts, stir once and turn into the pineapple 'boats'. Garnish with a sprinkling of spring onion rings and coriander leaves.

FRIED CURRIED RICE

KHAO PAD PONG KARI

*2tbsp/30ml oil
1 garlic clove, finely chopped
8oz/240g/2 cups plain boiled rice
2oz/60g/1 small potato, diced small
2oz/60g/1 small onion, diced small
2oz/60g/$^1/_4$cup peas
3tbsp/45ml light soy sauce
$^1/_2$tsp/2.5ml sugar
1tsp/5ml curry powder
$^1/_2$tsp/2.5ml ground white pepper*

*To garnish
1inch/2.5cm cucumber, finely sliced into rounds
coriander leaves*

In a wok or frying pan/skillet, heat the oil until a light haze appears, add the garlic and fry until golden brown. Add the boiled rice, stir once, add all the remaining ingredients and stir until thoroughly mixed. Turn on to a serving dish and garnish with cucumber rounds and coriander.

FRIED RICE WITH BASIL

KHAO PAD KRAPOW

Fried rice is the classic 'filler' and obviously the best solution to the inevitable leftover rice. This dish is the most famous version of all, found everywhere in Thailand and much appreciated for its chili heat. You can tone it down or heat it up depending on your tolerance. Surprisingly, the chili is a latecomer to oriental cuisine, brought by the Portuguese from South America probably in the late sixteenth century. Before that we perked up our flavours with mustard and pepper. Less surprisingly, we human beings are the only members of the animal kingdom who will touch the fiery little plant!

2tbsp/30ml oil
1 garlic clove, finely chopped
3 small fresh red or green chilis, finely chopped
3oz/90g/1 cup fresh button mushrooms, halved
1 small onion, chopped
8oz/240g/2 cups cooked rice
2oz/60g/1 small bundle long beans (or French/
snap beans),
cut into $^1/_2$inch/1.25cm pieces
2oz/60g/1 small red or green pepper, diced
$^1/_2$tsp/2.5ml sugar
3tbsp/45ml light soy sauce
15 sweet basil leaves

In a wok or frying pan/skillet, heat the oil until a light haze appears. Add the garlic and chilis and fry until the garlic is golden brown. Add the mushrooms and onions and stir quickly. Add the cooked rice and stir thoroughly. Add the long beans, peppers, sugar and light soy sauce and stir thoroughly. At the last moment quickly stir in the basil leaves and turn on to a serving dish.

GRILLED CURRIED RICE

KHAO NGOP

For this unusual recipe you will need red curry paste. There is a recipe for this on p. 105, but you can buy a ready-made version from an oriental store.

4fl oz/125ml/$^1/_2$cup coconut cream
1tsp/5ml red curry paste
2oz/60g/$^2/_3$cup pre-soaked Chinese dried
mushrooms, finely chopped
1oz/30g/$^1/_4$cup pea aubergines/eggplants (p. 56)
2oz/60g/about 4 whole baby sweetcorn
2oz/60g/1 small bundle long beans, coarsely
chopped
$^1/_2$tsp/2.5ml salt
2 kaffir lime leaves, finely chopped
10 sweet basil leaves
8oz/240g/2 cups plain boiled rice
$^1/_2$banana leaf, if available

Place the coconut cream in a large bowl and stir in the red curry paste until thoroughly blended. Add all the vegetables, stir well, add the salt, kaffir lime leaves and sweet basil leaves and stir. Add the boiled rice, stirring until thoroughly mixed. Turn this flavoured rice into the centre of the banana leaf (kitchen foil is a possible substitute). Fold the leaf into a square 'packet' around the rice and place under a hot grill/broiler, turning from time to time for a total of 8 minutes. Serve in the opened banana leaf.

NOODLES

After rice, noodles are the second great staple of oriental cuisine and another useful source of nutrition in the vegetarian diet. There are five main varieties of noodle.

Sen yai Sometimes called river rice noodle or rice sticks, this is a broad, flat, white noodle. Bought fresh, it is rather sticky and the strands usually need to be separated by hand before cooking. Sen yai can also be bought dried.

Ba mee An egg noodle, medium yellow in colour, which can be bought fresh in 'nests'; these need to be shaken loose by hand before cooking.

Sen mee A small wiry looking rice noodle, usually sold dried, sometimes called rice vermicelli.

Sen lek A medium flat noodle, about $\frac{1}{10}$ inch/2mm wide, and usually sold dried.

Wun sen A very thin, very wiry, transparent soya bean flour noodle, also called either vermicelli, or cellophane noodle. Only available dried.

All dried noodles need to be soaked in cold water for about 20 minutes before cooking; (vermicelli will usually require less soaking). They are quickly drained in a sieve or colander, and then cooked; usually a matter of simply dunking them in boiling water for 2–3 seconds. The dry weight will usually double after soaking, ie. 4oz/120g dry noodles are equivalent to 8oz/240g soaked noodles.

FOUR FLAVOURS

KRUANG PRUNG

While each noodle dish has a distinctive flavour of its own, the final taste is left very much up to the consumer. When eating noodles in Thailand, it is standard practice to offer a set of four dressings: Nam Pla Prik, chilis in fish sauce – though strict vegetarians can use light soy sauce instead – (4 small green or red chilis to 4tbsp/60ml fish sauce); Prik Nam Som, chopped chilis in rice vinegar (4 small green or red chilis to 4tbsp/60ml vinegar); Nam Tan, sugar; and Prik Pon, red chili powder; so that the dish can be adjusted as the diner wishes.

THAI FRIED NOODLES

GUEYTEOW PAD THAI Ⓔ

Thailand acquired the idea of making pasta dishes from the Chinese, thus noodles are one of the few dishes that we eat with chopsticks. Ease of preparation has made both dry (fried) and soup (boiled) noodles our favourite fast food, a standard lunch for the hard-pressed city dweller and a late night snack for those out on the town. Once thought to be a rather filling dish for the greedy, noodles have recently been restored to favour due to their fibre content – I just think of them as being very delicious. This recipe, Pad Thai, is considered our national dish because you can find it wherever we have settled. It is not only a fascinating mix of flavours but also an intriguing combination of textures – crunchy beansprouts and nuts, offset by the soft sen lek noodles.

3tbsp/43ml oil
1 garlic clove, finely chopped
2oz/60g/ $^1/_2$ cup ready-fried beancurd, cut into
$^1/_2$ inch/1.25 cm cubes
1 egg
4oz/120g dry sen lek noodles, soaked in water
for 20 minutes until soft, then drained
1tbsp/15ml chi po, preserved turnip, finely chopped
2 spring onions/scallions, cut into 1inch/2.5cm
pieces
2tbsp/30ml chopped roast peanuts
3oz/90g/$^2/_3$ cup beansprouts
$^1/_2$ tsp/2.5ml chili powder
1tsp/5ml sugar
2tbsp/30ml light soy sauce
1tbsp/15ml lemon juice

To garnish
sprig of coriander, coarsely chopped
1 lemon wedge

In a wok or frying pan/skillet, heat the oil until a light haze appears. Add the garlic and fry until golden brown. Add the ready-fried beancurd and stir briefly. Break the egg into the wok, cook for a moment then stir. Add the noodles, stir well, then add the preserved turnip and the spring onions along with half of the peanuts and half of the beansprouts. Stir well then add the chili powder, sugar, light soy sauce and lemon juice. Stir well and turn on to a plate. Sprinkle with the remaining peanuts and chopped coriander leaf. Arrange the remaining beansprouts (to be mixed in by the diner at the last moment) and the lemon wedge, on the side of the plate.

NOODLES WITH VEGETABLE AND CURRY SAUCE

GUEYTEOW PAK

This dish is a speciality of my friends Narind and Warochun at their restaurant The Lemon Grass, Sukhumvit Soi 24, Bangkok, certainly one of the best places to eat in that city. Narind is the chef and often creates new dishes or new versions of traditional ones. Not surprisingly, the restaurant, with its antique furniture and old photographs and paintings, is now internationally famous. Warochun tells me that they are more than happy to receive vegetarian diners and delighted to produce meat-free meals on request.

4oz/120g fresh white sen yai noodles
2oz/60g/^{1}/$_2$cup beansprouts
2oz/60g/1 small bundle long beans, chopped into
1 inch/2.5cm lengths
2oz/60g/1 medium broccoli stem, sliced lengthwise
8fl oz/250ml/1 cup coconut milk
1tbsp/15ml red curry paste (p. 105)
1tsp/5ml curry powder
^{1}/$_2$tsp/2.5ml salt
1tsp/5ml sugar
1tbsp/15ml tamarind juice
1tbsp/15ml roast peanuts, crushed
1 shallot, finely chopped

To garnish
potato rounds, extra-finely diced, deep-fried until
golden brown and set aside

In a large pan of boiling water, blanch the noodles and set aside. Blanch the beansprouts, long beans and broccoli stems, arrange on a serving dish and set aside.

In a saucepan, gently heat the coconut milk, stirring in the red curry paste until thoroughly blended. Add all the remaining ingredients, stirring until mixed. Turn into a serving bowl.

Either serve all three elements separately or place the noodles on the serving dish with the vegetables, pour over the sauce and garnish with the crispy potato.

FRIED NOODLES WITH BLACK FUNGUS MUSHROOMS

GUEYTEOW PAD SI EW Ⓔ

3tbsp/45ml oil
1 garlic clove, finely chopped
1oz/30g/^{1}/$_3$cup pre-soaked dried
black fungus mushrooms
1 egg
4oz/120g sen yai noodles, rinsed and separated
2oz/60g/1 medium stalk broccoli, coarsely chopped
1tsp/5ml dark soy sauce
1tbsp/15ml light soy sauce
^{1}/$_2$tsp/2.5ml sugar
1tsp/5ml white vinegar
^{1}/$_2$tsp/2.5ml chili powder
^{1}/$_2$tsp/2.5ml ground white pepper
1 large fresh red chili, finely chopped

In a wok or frying pan/skillet, heat the oil until a light haze appears. Add the garlic and fry until golden brown, break the egg into the wok and stir briefly, quickly adding the mushrooms, the noodles, broccoli, light and dark soy, sugar, vinegar, chili powder, pepper and red chili. Stir well. Turn on to a serving dish.

Noodles with vegetable and curry sauce

CURRY FLAVOURED MUSHROOM NOODLES

GUEYTEOW HET SAP

4 lettuce leaves (any variety)
3tbsp/45ml oil
4oz/120g sen yai noodles
1tsp/5ml dark soy sauce
1 garlic clove, finely chopped
3oz/90g/1 cup button mushrooms, chopped
1 small onion, chopped
1 tsp/5ml cornflour/cornstarch mixed with
4fl oz/125ml/ $^1/_2$cup vegetable
stock (p. 85) or water to make a thin paste
1tsp/5ml curry powder
$^1/_2$tsp/2.5ml sugar
2tbsp/30ml light soy sauce
a sprinkling of ground white pepper
1tsp/5ml tang chi, preserved radish

To garnish
sprig of coriander, coarsely chopped

Arrange the lettuce leaves on a serving dish and set aside. In a wok or frying pan/skillet, heat 1tbsp/15ml of the oil until a light haze appears. Add the noodles, stir, add the dark soy sauce, and stir well until the noodles are cooked al dente. Turn on to the lettuce and set aside.

Put the remaining oil into the wok, heat, add the garlic, and fry until golden brown. Add the mushrooms and onion, stir well. Pour in the thin flour paste, stir in the curry powder, add the sugar, light soy sauce, white pepper and preserved radish. Stir well, pour over the noodles, garnish with coriander and serve.

NOODLES WITH BLACK BEANS, SWEETCORN AND BROCCOLI

GUEYTEOW LAHD NAH

2 tbsp/30ml oil
4oz/120g sen mee noodles, soaked in water for
20 minutes until soft, then drained
1 garlic clove, finely chopped
1tsp/5ml black bean sauce
2oz/60g/1 medium stalk broccoli, cut into sprigs
2oz/60g/about 4 baby sweetcorn
1 large fresh red chili, finely chopped
$^1/_2$tsp/2.5ml sugar
2tbsp/30ml light soy sauce
1tsp/5ml cornflour/cornstarch, mixed with
4tbsp/60ml water to make a very thin paste
$^1/_2$tsp/2.5ml ground white
pepper
1tsp/5ml white vinegar

In a wok or frying pan/skillet, heat half the oil, add the noodles, stir quickly until just cooked, then turn on to a serving dish. Add the remaining oil to the wok and heat, then add the garlic and fry until golden brown. Add the black bean sauce, broccoli, baby sweetcorn, red chili, sugar and light soy sauce, and stir well. Pour in the flour and water paste, stir, add the pepper and vinegar, stir once, pour over noodles and serve.

CHIANG MAI CURRY NOODLES

KOW SOI Ⓔ

The history of relations between Burma and Thailand, or Siam as it used to be known, makes sorry reading – a story of successive conquests as each struggled to dominate the other, culminating in the Burmese invasion just over 200 years ago when they burned our capital Ayuthya and wiped out the royal dynasty. It was the resurrection of the nation around a little fishing port called Bangkok that launched modern Thailand. But while the Burmese have often been our enemies, there have always been close relations between the two peoples in the border area in the north of Thailand. The art and architecture of the ancient Kingdom of Chiang Mai shows the influence of Burmese styles and there are traces of the rich spiciness of Burmese cooking in some northern dishes, especially this one.

4oz/120g fresh ba me egg noodles dipped into boiling water
until cooked al dente, drained, turned into a bowl and set aside
2tbsp/30ml oil
1 garlic clove, finely chopped
1tsp/5ml red curry paste (p.105)
4fl oz/125ml/$^1/_2$cup coconut milk
2oz/60g/$^1/_2$cup ready-fried beancurd, chopped
8fl oz/250ml/1cup vegetable stock (p. 85) or water
1tsp/5ml curry powder
$^1/_4$tsp/1.5ml turmeric powder
3tbsp/45ml light soy sauce
$^1/_2$tsp/2.5ml sugar
1tbsp/15ml lemon juice

To garnish
1 spring onion/scallion, coarsely chopped
2 shallots, finely diced
1tbsp/15ml pickled cabbage (tinned Thai/Chinese)
coriander leaves
1 lemon, cut into wedges

In a wok or frying pan/skillet, heat the oil until a light haze appears. Fry the garlic until golden. Add the curry paste, mix in and cook for a few seconds. Add the coconut milk, mix in and cook until the liquid starts to reduce. Add the beancurd and stir thoroughly, then add the stock, curry powder, turmeric, light soy, sugar and lemon juice, stirring after each addition. Cook over a high heat, stirring constantly, for about 10 seconds. Pour the mixture over the noodles, garnish and serve.

DRUNKARD'S NOODLES

GUEYTEOW PAD KI MOW

This is a favourite hangover dish – the chilis kick-start the benumbed body while the lime leaf refreshes and clears the jaded palate.

2tbsp/30ml oil
1 garlic clove, finely chopped
2 small fresh red or green chilis, finely chopped
4oz/12g sen yai noodles
1 small onion, cut into segments
1 medium tomato, cut into segments
4 kaffir lime leaves, roughly chopped
6 sweet basil leaves
1tsp/5ml dark soy sauce
2tbsp/30ml light soy sauce
$^1/_2$tsp/2.5ml sugar
2oz/60g/1 small sweet red or green pepper, finely chopped

In a wok or frying pan/skillet, heat the oil until a light haze appears. Add the garlic and chilis and fry until the garlic is golden brown. Add the noodles, stir, add the remaining ingredients and stir well until the peppers begin to cook but are still al dente. Turn on to a dish.

DEEP-FRIED NOODLES WITH MIXED VEGETABLES

GO SEE MEE Ⓔ

If you visit Yaowaraj, Bangkok's Chinese quarter, you will be dazzled by the neon-lit shops of the gold merchants hung about with countless glittering gold chains. You can often find an egg noodle seller in front of these shops and I am always amused by the way the chains of yellow noodles hanging in the glass fronted cabinet are like a poor man's version of all that gold. The glass cabinets are mounted on little wagons that are pushed up and down the busy streets. The noodles are precooked: when you place your order the vegetables are quickly stir-fried and the sauce is poured over the crispy golden brown curls.

1 nest of egg noodles
oil for deep-frying

Separate the strands of egg noodle. Heat the oil and fry the noodles until crisp. Remove and drain. Place on a serving dish and set aside.

2tbsp/30ml oil
1 garlic clove, finely chopped
2oz/60g/ $^1/_2$ cup bamboo shoots, finely sliced
2oz/60g/ $^2/_3$ cup straw mushrooms
2oz/60g/about 4 baby sweetcorn, cut in half lengthwise
2oz/60g/1 small sweet red or green pepper, diced
2 spring onions/scallions chopped into 1inch/2.5cm lengths
2tbsp/30ml light soy sauce
1tsp/15ml dark soy sauce
1tsp/5ml sugar
$^1/_2$tsp/2.5ml ground white pepper
1tbsp/15ml cornflour/cornstarch mixed with
4fl oz/125ml/ $^1/_2$ cup vegetable stock (p. 85) or water to make a thin paste

To garnish
coriander leaves

In a wok or frying pan/skillet, heat the oil until a light haze appears. Fry the garlic until golden brown. Add all the remaining ingredients, stirring constantly and finally stirring in the thin flour paste. Pour over the crispy egg noodles, garnish with coriander and serve.

FRIED EGG NOODLES WITH BEAN-CURD

BA MEE PAD Ⓔ

1 nest egg noodles dipped in boiling water until cooked al dente, then drained
3tbsp/45ml oil
1 garlic clove, finely chopped
1 egg
2oz/60g/ $^1/_2$ cup ready-fried beancurd, chopped into $^1/_2$ inch/2.5cm cubes
1tbsp/15ml chi po, preserved turnip, finely chopped
2tbsp/30ml chopped roast peanuts
$^1/_2$tsp/2.5ml chili powder
1tsp/5ml sugar
2tbsp/30ml light soy sauce
1tbsp/15ml lemon juice
2oz/60g/ $^1/_2$ cup beansprouts
2 spring onions/scallions, coarsely chopped

Heat the oil and fry the garlic until golden brown. Break the egg into the oil, leave to cook for a moment then stir, quickly adding the beancurd then the cooked noodles. Add the chi po, half the roast peanuts, the chili powder, sugar, soy sauce, lemon juice, half the beansprouts and half the spring onions, stirring constantly. Be sure that the vegetables remain al dente. Turn on to a serving dish and arrange the remaining peanuts, beansprouts and spring onions on the side of the dish to be mixed in by the diner.

Thai fried noodles and deep-fried noodles with mixed vegetables

EGG NOODLES WITH CHILI AND LEMON

Ba mee so ba Ⓔ

1tbsp/15ml roast peanuts, lightly crushed
1tbsp/15ml sesame seeds
1 nest fresh egg noodles
2 small red or green chilis, finely chopped
2 tbsp/30ml lemon juice
1 garlic clove, finely chopped
1tbsp/15ml cooking oil
3tbsp/45ml light soy sauce
1tsp/5ml sugar
1oz/30g/$\frac{1}{2}$cup white cabbage, finely chopped
1oz/30g/1 stalk celery, finely chopped
1oz/30g/1 carrot, finely chopped
1oz/30g/$\frac{1}{3}$cup beansprouts
1oz/30g/$\frac{1}{3}$cup pre-soaked dried black fungus mushrooms, finely chopped
2inch/5cm piece ginger root, peeled and cut into fine matchsticks

To garnish
1 spring onion/scallion, finely chopped into white and green rings
coriander leaves

Set aside the lightly crushed peanuts. Dry-fry the sesame seeds until golden brown and set aside.

Shake the strands of fresh egg noodle free. Bring a pan of water to the boil. Using a coarse-meshed strainer or sieve, dip the noodles into the boiling water for approximately one minute until cooked al dente. Set aside.

Soak the chilis in the lemon juice and set aside. Fry the garlic in the oil until golden brown then add all the vegetables and stir-fry.

Tip the vegetables over the noodles in a mixing bowl, add all the other ingredients except for the garnish, mix thoroughly, then turn on to a serving dish. Garnish with a spring onion and coriander leaves.

CHILIS

Given how chili-hot much Southeast Asian food is, it comes as something of a surprise to learn that the fiery little devils are a fairly recent addition to our cuisine, having been brought from South America by the Portuguese in the sixteenth century.

A rough rule is that the smaller the hotter, though no batch is exactly the same and a true Thai cook has a little nibble to test before buying in quantity, something not to be tried by newcomers to hot food. Also, do be wary after handling chilis: be sure to wash your hands well before touching the sensitive parts of the body.

If the seeds of the chili are removed, the heat is effectively cancelled, and only the taste of the chili remains. Unless otherwise stated, do not remove the seeds for these recipes, unless you cannot tolerate hot food.

Three sorts of chili are needed for the recipes in this book:
- Small fresh red and green chilis which are very hot and virtually identical except for colour. There is also a small yellow variety, seldom seen in the West.
- Large fresh red or green chilis, which are much milder.
- Large dried red chilis, which are milder still.

RICE NOODLES WITH COCONUT

MEE GRAT TI

As with many of the best dishes from other cuisines – the pastas of Italy and the bean dishes of France – this recipe is a product of poverty. In Thailand these ingredients are cheap and readily available. The qualities of the dish come from the ingenuity with which the flavours of such ordinary (to us!) materials are blended. The use of coconut in cooking is typically Thai and Burmese and is little known in China. In this dish its rich, creamy flavour is used to best effect.

4oz/120g dry sen mee noodles soaked in water for
about 20 minutes
2 small shallots
8 black peppercorns
1 large red chili
$^1/_2$tsp/2.5ml salt
6tbsp/90ml coconut cream (p. 152)
3tbsp/45ml vegetable stock (p. 85) or water
1tsp/5ml sugar
$^1/_2$tsp/2.5ml chili powder
2tbsp/30ml light soy sauce
2oz/60g/$^1/_2$cup ready-fried beancurd, sliced into thin
squares
4oz/120g/1$^1/_4$cups beansprouts
1 spring onion/scallion, finely chopped

To garnish
coriander leaves

Put the shallots, peppercorns, chili and salt into a mortar, pound until a paste forms then set aside.

In a pan, heat the coconut cream and stir in the vegetable stock or water, the sugar, chili powder and light soy sauce. Next add the paste from the mortar, stirring

until all the ingredients are blended together. Strain the noodles, put into the sauce and cook until al dente. When the noodles are almost cooked add the beancurd, beansprouts and spring onion, mix and turn on to a serving dish. Garnish with coriander leaves.

EGG NOODLES WITH STIR-FRY VEGETABLES

MEE SUA Ⓔ

For this dish you will need to find an oriental store, say a Chinese supermarket or similar emporium with a refrigerated section where you should be able to find cellophane packets of ready-cooked egg noodles. They should be chilled not frozen and look bright yellow, plump and shiny.

2tbsp/30ml oil
1 garlic clove, finely chopped
1 large red dry chili, roughly chopped
4oz/120g/1 cup ready-cooked egg noodles
2oz/60g/1 stalk celery, finely chopped
2oz/60g/$^1/_2$cup beansprouts
2 spring onions/scallions, finely chopped
1 medium tomato, cut into segments
$^1/_2$tsp/2.5ml chili powder
3tbsp/45ml light soy sauce
1tsp/5ml dark soy sauce
$^1/_2$tsp/2.5ml sugar

In a wok, heat the oil until a light haze appears. Fry the garlic, after a moment add the chili and continue stir-frying until the garlic is golden. Add the noodles, stir well, then add all the remaining ingredients, stirring quickly. Turn on to a serving dish.

Nam prik curry noodles

Kanom jin nam prik

This recipe requires a fresh white noodle which is made only on special occasions in Thailand. Normally noodles are made in the Chinese way from a dough which is teased or pulled out as if winding wool. This noodle, however, is made by squeezing the dough through a sieve into boiling water and then rapidly cooling it in order to preserve the shape until needed for cooking – usually the following day. This labour is usually undertaken by large groups of people on feast days – I last saw it done by the adults of an entire village who were preparing a feast for the great annual ceremony held during the rainy season when some of the boys become monks.

Happily for the Western cook, similar noodles are available in oriental stores: they are round, white, resemble spaghetti and are called longxu. Many different vegetables may be used but I have suggested three types more readily available in the west.

The noodles and vegetables
8oz/240g white longxu noodles
4oz/120g/1 bundle long beans, finely chopped
4oz/120g/1 bundle morning glory, roughly chopped
4oz/120g/1 ¼ cups bean sprouts

Boil the cluster of noodle until al dente. Drain and dip for a moment into cold water to stop the cooking. Drain and place on a serving dish.

Bring a pan of fresh water to the boil and blanch each of the vegetables in turn, keeping them al dente. Drain and place in their clusters around the dish.

Nam Prik Sauce
4tbsp/60ml oil
10 shallots, finely sliced into rings
5 garlic cloves, finely chopped

4fl oz/125ml/½ cup dried split moong beans, soaked in water for 6 hours
2 coriander roots
1tbsp/15ml red curry paste (p. 105)
2pints/1 ¼ cups coconut milk
2tbsp/30ml light soy sauce
1tbsp/15ml sugar
1tbsp/15ml tamarind juice
1tbsp/15ml lemon juice
½tsp/2.5ml chili powder
1 kaffir lime, cut in half
8fl oz/250ml/1 cup water

Heat 2tbsp/30ml of the oil until a light haze forms, then fry half the shallots and half the garlic until crispy brown. Drain and set aside, keeping the oil for the Fried Dry Chilis (below).

Drain the moong beans, place in a mortar, pound well to form a paste and set aside. In the mortar, pound together the coriander roots with the remaining shallots and garlic until a paste forms, then set aside. In a frying pan or wok heat the remaining unused oil, stir in the red curry paste and cook. Add half the coconut milk, stirring well, add the paste of coriander root, shallot and garlic and thoroughly mix. Add in the moong bean paste and stir well. Add the soy sauce, sugar and tamarind juice, lemon juice and chili powder, stirring constantly. Put the two halves of the kaffir lime into the mixture and continue to cook gently. Thin the remaining coconut milk with the water then stir into the sauce and boil. Simmer for 1 minute. Quickly stir in the crispy shallot and garlic mix and immediately turn into a serving bowl. Save the remaining oil for the side dish.

Fried Dry Chilis
2 large dried red chilis, coarsely chopped
the reserved oil from the sauce recipe

Re-heat the oil and quickly stir-fry the chilis. Turn into a small serving bowl. Serves three.

Nam Prik Curry Noodles

This is one of the few Thai dishes that does not have to be eaten hot. Suitable for parties, it is often served as three separate dishes, which guests can mix. This version is chili hot!

35

SOUTHERN SALAD

SALAD KAEK

Kaek is the colloquial word for a muslim from the south of Thailand, near our border with Malaysia. The Kaeks introduced the southern nut-flavoured sauces into our cuisine, in dishes such as satay, which originated in Malaysia, but has been adapted to Thai tastes. This salad also shows their influence and is very rich and filling.

Prepare a mixed salad of lettuce, onion, cucumber, beansprout and tomato and set aside.

The sauce
2tbsp/30ml oil
1 garlic clove, finely chopped
1tsp/5ml red curry paste (p. 105)
2oz/60g/$^1/_3$cup coconut cream (p. 152)
2tbsp/30ml crushed roast peanuts
1tsp/5ml sugar
3tbsp/45ml light soy sauce
2tbsp/30ml lemon juice
3tbsp/45ml vegetable stock (p. 85)

To garnish
2oz/60g/$^1/_2$cup ready-fried beancurd, chopped
into 1inch/2.5cm cubes
2 medium potatoes, sliced wafer thin and deep-fried
until crisp (or a packet of potato crisps/chips)

Heat the oil, fry the garlic golden brown, add the curry paste and stir briefly. Add the coconut cream and boil, stirring well. Add the other ingredients, mixing well. Remove from heat and allow to cool.

Either pour this sauce over the salad and garnish with beancurd cubes and potato crisps (do not mix, this will be done by the diners), or serve each element separately so that the diners can mix as they choose on their own plates.

FRIED BATTERED MUSHROOMS WITH BEANSPROUTS

PAD HET MALANG Ⓔ

The batter
2tbsp/30ml potato flour
2tbsp/30ml flour
$^1/_2$tsp/2.5ml salt
8tbsp/120ml water
4oz/120g/1 $^1/_3$cups whole straw mushrooms

In a bowl, mix the two flours, the salt and water to make a batter. Mix in the mushrooms and set aside.

The other ingredients
2tbsp/30ml oil
1 garlic clove, finely chopped
1 egg
4oz/120g/1 $^1/_4$cups fresh beansprouts
2 spring onions/scallions, finely sliced into rings
2tbsp/30ml light soy sauce
1tsp/5ml dark soy sauce
1tsp/5ml sugar
sprinkling of ground white pepper

To garnish
coriander leaves

In a frying pan/skillet (preferably non-stick), heat the oil until a light haze appears. Fry the garlic until golden. Pour the mushroom and batter mix into the pan as if it were an omelette. Fry until the underside is crisp but the interior is still soft. When just solid enough, cut this pancake with a sharp knife into large squares and quickly turn them over to fry the uncooked upper side. When nearly crisp break the egg into the pan and stir well, then quickly stir in all the remaining ingredients and turn on to a serving dish.

What you will have is a dish of stir-fried beansprouts and spring onions/scallions, with solid chunks of battered mushroom not unlike squares of ready-fried beancurd. Garnish with the coriander and serve with either hot Sriracha Chili Sauce (p. 11) or Prik Nam Som (p. 25).

Fried battered mushrooms with beansprouts

WHITE RADISH CAKE WITH BEANSPROUTS

KANOM PAD GA TUA NGOK Ⓔ

This recipe is prepared in two distinct stages: first the cake is made, then it is re-cooked with beansprouts, as here, or with other ingredients. It will serve 3–4.

For the cake
1 mooli, white radish, weighing about 2lb/1kg
6oz/180g/1 $^1/_2$ cups rice flour
2tbsp/30ml wheat flour
2tbsp/30ml water

Trim and peel the radish and cut into small cubes. Using a food processor or blender, mash the radish as finely as possible. This will have to be done in 2–3 batches. Mix the radish thoroughly with the rice and wheat flours and the water. Turn the mixture into a shallow tin or heatproof dish, about 8inches/20cm square: it should come about 1inch/2.5cm up the sides. Heat up your steamer (or use your largest sauce-pan with an upturned bowl in the bottom on which to rest the tin) and steam the cake for about 30 minutes from the time the steamer is hot. If you are using a thicker dish you will have to steam it for a little longer. When an inserted knife comes out clean, remove from the heat and allow to cool and dry out completely. It will set more solidly as it cools. Cut the cake into rectangles, about 1×2inches/2.5×5cm.

To finish
3 tbsp/45ml oil
$^1/_2$ batch white radish cakes, cut into rectangles as above
2 garlic cloves, finely chopped
1 egg
2tbsp/30ml light soy sauce
1tsp/5ml dark soy sauce
$^1/_2$ tsp/2.5ml sugar
ground white pepper
1oz/30g/ $^1/_3$ cup fresh beansprouts, rinsed and drained
3 spring onions/scallions, cut into 1inch/2.5cm slivers

In a frying pan/skillet (preferably non-stick), heat half the oil. Add the radish cake pieces and, stirring and turning constantly, fry until they are browned on all sides. Remove from the pan and set aside. Add the rest of the oil and re-heat. Add the garlic and fry until golden brown. Break in the egg, stir to mix and cook for a few seconds until the egg starts to set. Add the reserved fried radish cake and mix thoroughly. Quickly add both soy sauces, the sugar, pepper, beansprouts and spring onions. Mix quickly and thoroughly. Turn on to a serving dish.

The remaining radish cake can be fried with other ingredients. This dish goes well with Prik Nam Som (p. 25) or Sriracha Chili Sauce (p. 11).

White radish cake with beansprouts

YAM: PIQUANT THAI SALADS

THE FOREST TEMPLE

The visitor to Thailand quickly becomes familiar with the country's most prominent architectural feature, the breathtaking red and gold temples that dominate the skyline of even the smallest towns. Each temple is a dazzling work of art, often blessed with intricate carved panels and fabulous painted murals. Beneath the sweeping, prow-like roof, under a vaulted ceiling, a huge gilded statue of the Buddha smiles serenely on saffron-robed monks and prostrate worshippers making their offerings of flowers and incense.

But there is another sort of Thai temple, virtually unknown to the visitor and, until recently, almost completely ignored by the city-dweller – the simple wooden temples, set in forest glades out in the countryside, away from the noise and smell of the modern world. Such forest temples are places of natural beauty and holiness. The buildings seem part of nature itself – the wooden pillars merging with the living trees as if the temple had grown rather than been built by men. The only signs of human agency are the carved entrances and the way the broadly planked floors have been polished by the feet of generations of worshippers. In

Basic yam ingredients

41

the half-light through shuttered windows, a folk-carved and painted Buddha, so different from his golden cousin in the city temple, meditates to the distant sounds of birds and insects, the signs of a living nature which make it easier to contemplate the inner truths of a faith that are often drowned amid the impenetrable traffic and soaring office blocks of modern Asia. Little wonder then, that increasing numbers of people are turning to the forest temples as a way of regenerating their inner life and as an antidote to the stresses of modern living. Many now choose to make a retreat, living in the temple compound in a basic tent, enjoying spiritual exercises in the total calm of the monastery farms and surrounding forest. Some of these temples now encourage vegetarianism, offering meat-free meals to their visitors. This is not an obligatory feature of Buddhism, rather a way of building a closer affinity with nature and all its forms of life.

Not all forest temples are lost in the deepest countryside. One such, Wat Sankatan, is only an hour's drive north of Bangkok on a broad woodland estate near a tributary of the Chao Phya river close to the town of Nonthaburi. More than 200 years older than the capital, Nonthaburi is divided by the river and is sometimes called the 'broken-hearted' town, after a city in the north of the country which is similarly split in two. This is the province of the durian, Asia's unique odiferous fruit (p. 145), and the temple grounds are dotted with durian trees as well as a vast collection of herbal and medicinal plants. When I visited the temple, the Abbot, the venerable Sanong, took me on a tour of the shaded avenues where, in tiny stilt-houses set among the plants and bushes, the monks live as close to nature as possible. The Abbot pointed out to me the

In a forest temple, a young monk meditates beside the body of a deceased colleague

Cultivating mushrooms at Wat Sankatan

'Dragon's Tongue' plant, a soup of which is good for bruises – he made me taste the leaf which is at once horribly bitter and curiously sweet. Then we came to the 'Mongoose Spit' plant – the juice of its leaves is mixed with whisky to make a cure for snake-bite!

The monks at Wat Sankatan are followers of the Maha Nikay or 'Great School', the original Buddhism that flourished in Thailand before the nineteenth-century reformation, and their sect is especially concerned with the natural cycle of life and death, as I was to learn. The Abbot led me down a distant path where there was a slightly larger stilt-house containing white boxes that I knew at once to be coffins. Here, in the presence of their deceased colleagues, the monks come to undertake the ultimate stage of their monastic study, Asupakamatan, the meditation on the decomposition of the human body. First the five external elements, skin, nails, teeth, the hair of the head and the hair of the body are studied, and then come the usually hidden inner elements, now exposed in the coffins. Did I, the Abbot enquired, wish to see inside one of the boxes? No, I did not, and thankfully we progressed to a series of long low barns where in damp darkness the monks cultivate mushrooms.

This is a valuable source of income for the monastery and is a fascinating mix of traditional skills and modern techniques. The mushrooms grown are nang rom, these are oyster mushrooms, similar to the pleurotte mushrooms of Europe. The first spoors are cultivated in bottles of agar jelly, then transferred to bottles of millet where, over fifteen days, a culture forms. In the meantime sawdust from rubber trees is sterilized in an oven, then mixed with mineral salts, glucose, beans and rice husks, to which a tiny amount of mushroom culture is added. The whole mix is stuffed into foot-long plastic cylinders and stacked in the dimly-lit huts with one end of the roll left open, and from here the startling white mushroom fronds begin to appear. It is a remarkable sight to see the weird ivory shoots blossoming in such profusion.

These mushrooms are very important in Thai vegetarian cooking as their texture and bulk make them an excellent substitute for meat. They also dry easily which adds to their convenience. The nang rom mushroom is especially good in a 'yam' dish, creating that blend of the pungent and the tongue-tingling which is the most typical of all Thai flavours. Yam dishes are unique to Thai cooking: the word means something akin to salad, but also includes lightly cooked vegetables. (It should not be confused with the African yam or sweet potato.) Yam dishes are a kaleidoscope of strong flavours – sour lemon and very hot chili, balanced by saltiness and sugar sweetness. The taste is essentially sharp and because of this, yam dishes are often brought out just ahead of the main meal as an accompaniment to drinks – they go very well with strong spirits.

There are two sorts of yam: I have chosen to put tom yam, the liquid variety, into the chapter on soups, and it is the dry variety that is featured here. There are hundreds of variations on the basic yam recipe, and the nineteen in this chapter show the possible range, from salad yams to those made with noodles and fruit. Although presented here in a chapter on their own, yam dishes are part of the main meal, even when sneaked out first, and are really too hot to be used as single dish meals without a generous helping of rice.

Now when I eat mushroom yam, my thoughts turn back to Wat Sankatan, though I try to concentrate on the avenues of trees and the pleasant sight of flowering mushrooms in the shady huts, rather than the distant stilt-house and its open white boxes with their proof of the natural cycle in which we are all inescapably linked.

MUSHROOMS

The firmness and texture of mushrooms make them a useful addition to many vegetarian dishes and I have used them often in this book. For ease I have suggested only the six commonly available varieties, though these are obviously not as flavourful as many of the wild mushrooms. If you are a competent gatherer of mushrooms or can occasionally get the wild ones in your market then you can adapt these recipes to the varieties you have found.

Dried black fungus mushrooms (Cloud Ears or Champignons noirs) These are the commonest Asian mushroom, usually bought dried in 2oz/60g packets. They should be soaked in water

Salad of black fungus mushrooms (p. 47) and hot and sour mushroom soup (p. 87)

at room temperature until soft (20–30 minutes). The smaller the mushrooms the better, and do remember to test any new brand you buy to be sure it is free of sandy grit.

Chinese dried mushrooms (Shiitake) These are almost the same shape as the common Western large flat mushroom, though they are slightly smaller and tougher in texture. They should be soaked in water at room temperature for about 20 minutes, the water squeezed out and the tough stalk removed. (Add the stalks to your vegetable stockpot, see p. 85.)

Champignons and button mushrooms Although technically different, these two varieties of young common cultivated mushrooms are interchangeable for culinary purposes. I refer to button mushrooms throughout, but you may use champignons de Paris wherever they occur.

Large flat mushroom (parasol mushroom) The commonest of the large fresh varieties in the West, they should always be firm and cleaned only by wiping with a damp cloth. The stems are usually tender enough to eat.

Oyster mushroom (pleurotte) Although the least common of the mushrooms mentioned here, fresh oyster mushrooms are occasionally available in oriental stores. However, substitutes are suggested.

Straw mushroom Softer and more pointed in shape than the button mushroom, these are much used by oriental cooks in the West because they remain reasonably firm when tinned.

OYSTER MUSHROOM YAM

YAM POW HOO

This is a very quick and easy dish to make and will teach you the basic yam sauce which you can then adapt to suit other vegetables. Because it is served on lettuce it makes ideal finger food to serve with drinks.

4oz/120g/1 1/3 cups oyster mushrooms
4tbsp/60ml vegetable stock (p. 85)
1/4 stalk/1 inch lemon grass, finely chopped
2 kaffir lime leaves, finely chopped
2 small red or green chilis, finely chopped
1/2 tsp/2.5ml chili powder
2tbsp/30ml lemon juice
3tbsp/45ml light soy sauce
1tsp/5ml sugar

To serve
4 or 5 crisp lettuce leaves
10 or 12 whole mint leaves

Form the lettuce leaves into a shallow 'bowl' on a serving dish and set aside. Pull apart the 'bouquet' of oyster mushrooms into 'leaves' of about 2inches/5cm. Plunge the mushrooms into rapidly boiling water, leave for one minute then remove and strain. Heat the stock in a saucepan, add the mushrooms, then all the other ingredients, and stir quickly for one minute until thoroughly mixed. Turn into the prepared 'bowl' and garnish with mint leaves.

Offerings of saffron robes and alms bowls in a village temple where the young men will become monks for a short period

SALAD OF BLACK FUNGUS MUSHROOMS

YAM HET HOO NOO

1 garlic clove
3 small red or green chilis
1tsp/5ml sugar
2tbsp/30ml lemon juice
2tbsp/30ml light soy sauce
2oz/60g/2/3 cup pre-soaked dried black fungus mushrooms, cut finely into thin strips
2oz/60g/1 stalk celery, chopped lengthways into 1inch/2.5cm matchsticks
1oz/30g/1 carrot, chopped lengthways into 1inch/2.5cm matchsticks
1oz/30g/1 small chunk cucumber, chopped lengthways into 1inch/2.5cm matchsticks
2 spring onions/scallions, chopped lengthways into 1inch/2.5cm matchsticks
1tbsp/15ml crushed roast peanuts
1tsp/5ml sesame seeds, dry-fried until 'roasted'
1 shallot, finely chopped into rings
4 or 5 lettuce leaves

To garnish
coriander leaves

In a mortar, pound the garlic and chili until well crushed. Combine with the sugar, lemon juice and soy to make a sauce and set aside.

In a bowl place the mushrooms, celery, carrot, cucumber and spring onions. Pour the sauce over the vegetables and stir well. Add the peanuts, sesame seeds and shallot rings and stir briefly. Arrange the lettuce leaves on a serving dish and place the mixture on them. Garnish with coriander leaves.

EIGHT HEROES YAM

YAM POY SIEN

This is a vegetarian version of the classic oriental dish Eight Heroes, which includes eight different sorts of meat. This dish, like the original, looks as dramatic as it tastes, and if served as suggested adds a dash of culinary showmanship to a dinner party. It takes a surprisingly small amount of each ingredient to produce this dish. Because everything has to be very finely shredded much is produced from little.

The garnish
1oz/30g/1 small potato
oil for deep-frying
1tbsp/15ml sesame seeds
1tbsp/15ml roast peanuts

The Eight Heroes
1oz/30g/$\frac{1}{2}$cup of each of the following vegetables, cut or shredded into very thin strips: red cabbage, white cabbage, mooli (white radish), celery, carrot, cucumber, spring onion/scallion
1oz/30g/$\frac{1}{3}$cup pre-soaked dried black fungus mushrooms

The yam
4tbsp/60ml vegetable stock (p. 85)
2 red or green peppers, finely chopped
3tbsp/45ml light soy sauce
2tbsp/30ml lemon juice
1tsp/5ml sugar
1 clove pickled garlic, finely chopped

Cut the potatoes into very thin slices, deep-fry until hard and golden brown and set aside. Dry fry the sesame seeds until brown and set aside. Lightly pound the peanuts until just crumbled – do not reduce to powder. Set aside.

Arrange the seven vegetables (not the mushrooms) in stripes on a serving platter. The aim is to make an attractive 'flag' of different colours so that you can set the dish as a table centrepiece.

In a saucepan heat the stock and add the mushrooms. Stir quickly then add the other yam ingredients. Stir until thoroughly mixed, then turn into a serving bowl.

Take the yam sauce and the garnishes to the table. Each diner tosses the vegetables with the sauce and takes a helping of garnish.

BROCCOLI STEM YAM

YAM KANAR

3 small red or green chilis
1 garlic clove
2tbsp/30ml light soy sauce
2tbsp/30ml lemon juice
1tsp/5ml sugar
2oz/60g/4 young broccoli stems, chopped diagonally into 1inch/2.5cm lengths
1oz/30g/1 young carrot, finely chopped into matchsticks
1oz/30g/1 small piece mooli, white radish, finely chopped into matchsticks
1oz/30g/$\frac{1}{3}$cup red cabbage, finely chopped

To garnish
2 small shallots and 1 garlic clove, finely chopped into rings and fried in 2tbsp/30ml oil until golden brown, then drained

In a mortar, pound the chilis and garlic, add the soy sauce, lemon juice and sugar and mix together. Place all the vegetables in a bowl, and pour over the yam sauce. Stir well, turn into a serving dish and garnish with fried shallot and garlic rings.

Broccoli stem yam

STICKY RICE

This is not, as you might imagine, rice that has gone wrong. Glutinous rice is a special variety of rice that does not dry and separate upon cooking but has a higher starch content which causes the grains to stick together slightly. It is essential to northern Thai cooking where it is the staple of the region, and the sweet variety is the basis of several Thai desserts. To make sticky rice:

1lb/450g/2 cups glutinous rice

Put the rice in a bowl, cover with cold water and soak for at least 3 hours. Drain and rinse thoroughly. Line the perforated part of a steamer with a double layer of muslin or cheesecloth and turn the rice into it. Heat water in the base and steam the rice for 30 minutes. Turn into a bowl and serve.

SOUTHERN-STYLE YAM

YAM TOWAI

The south of Thailand, lying between the Andaman Sea and the Gulf of Thailand, has only recently been added to the visitors' itinerary. Its once deserted islands have become the favoured destination of the young, who go there to lead an idyllic beachcombing existence on very little money. Inevitably the tourist hotels are beginning to catch up but there is still many a tiny fishing village untouched by development. The food of southern Thailand is notoriously hot. On the border with Malaysia, Thailand's Muslim minority have introduced richer curry flavours reminiscent of Indian food, which they prefer to the thin soup-like curries made elsewhere in Thailand. This southern-style yam has echoes of those influences.

The yam
8–10 button mushrooms, sliced to retain the mushroom outline
2×4tbsp/60ml coconut cream (p. 152)
1tbsp/15ml cooking oil
1tsp/5ml red curry paste (p. 105)
2tbsp vegetable stock (p. 85)
1tsp/5ml turmeric powder
2tsp/10ml tamarind juice
1tsp/5ml lemon juice
4tbsp/60ml light soy sauce
1tsp/5ml sugar

The vegetables
1oz/30g/$^{1}/_{3}$cup each of beansprouts, morning glory, bamboo shoots, long beans, roughly cut to the length of the beansprouts
2oz/60g/$^{1}/_{2}$ small green aubergine/eggplant (p. 56), quartered

The garnish
2 shallots, finely chopped
1tbsp/15ml oil
1tbsp/15ml sesame seeds, dry-fried until golden

Put the mushrooms and the first measure of coconut cream in a saucepan, bring almost to the boil then set aside.

Heat the oil, add the red curry paste, then after a moment stir in the stock and the second measure of coconut cream. Add the remaining yam ingredients. Stir in the prepared mushrooms with coconut cream. Set aside.

Plunge each of the vegetables in turn into a large pan of boiling water, blanch, drain and arrange in radiating lines on a large circular serving dish. For the garnish, fry the shallots in the oil until golden. At the last moment pour the yam sauce, then the shallot oil over the vegetables. Finally scatter over the sesame seeds and serve.

MANY VEGETABLES SALAD

YAM YAI

The salad
4 or 5 lettuce leaves
1oz/30g/1 small onion, sliced into rings
1oz/30g/1 small chunk cucumber
1oz/30g/1 stalk celery, finely chopped
1oz/30g/1 young carrot, finely chopped
1oz/30g/^{1}/$_2$small red and green sweet pepper, finely chopped
1 medium sized tomato, sliced into rounds
1oz/30g/^{1}/$_3$cup raw button mushrooms, halved

Decoratively arrange all the above in a large salad bowl and set aside.

The yam
1tsp/5ml sesame seeds
4tbsp/60ml vegetable stock (p. 85) or water
2oz/60g clear vermicelli, soaked in water until soft, drained and cut into 2inch/5cm lengths
3 small red or green chilis, finely chopped
4tbsp/60ml light soy sauce
3tbsp/45ml lemon juice
1tsp/5ml sugar
1 head of pickled garlic, finely chopped
1tbsp/15ml pickling vinegar (from the garlic pickle)
1tbsp/15ml ground roast peanuts
2oz/60g/^{1}/$_2$cup ready-fried beancurd, finely chopped

To garnish
coriander leaves

In a dry frying pan/skillet, toss the sesame seeds until 'roasted' and set aside.

In a large pan, bring the stock to the boil, add the noodles, chili, soy sauce, lemon juice and sugar, stir quickly and remove from heat. Add the pickled garlic and the pickling vinegar, stir. Add the roast peanuts, bean curd and sesame seeds, stir. Pour over the salad, garnish with coriander leaves and serve.

SPICY MIXED VEGETABLE SALAD

YAM PAK RUAM MIT

1oz/30g/about 1 large leaf Chinese cabbage roughly chopped diagonally across the leaf
1oz/30g/about 2 baby sweetcorn, roughly chopped into circles
1oz/30g/1 young carrot, finely chopped into matchsticks
1oz/30g/^{1}/$_3$cup fresh button mushrooms, finely sliced
1oz/30g/^{1}/$_3$cup pre-soaked dried black fungus mushrooms, finely chopped
1oz/30g/1 stalk celery (stem and leaf), finely chopped
1 garlic clove, finely chopped
4 small red or green chilis, finely chopped
2tbsp/30ml light soy sauce
2tbsp/30ml lemon juice
1tsp/5ml sugar
1tsp/5ml sesame seeds, dry-fried until golden

To garnish
1 medium sized tomato, cut into segments
10 mint leaves

Bring a large pan of water to the boil and briefly plunge in the Chinese cabbage, sweetcorn, carrots, both types of mushroom, and celery. Drain, place in a bowl, then add all the other ingredients, stirring well. Turn on to a serving dish and garnish with the tomato segments and mint leaves.

HOT AND SOUR VERMICELLI SALAD
YAM WUN SEN

Although this is a substantial dish the fact that the noodle element is made from beans and not flour means that it is not fattening. Indeed Thai women often use vermicelli noodles as a substitute for rice when dieting. The pleasure of this recipe is the contrast between the rather bland slippery noodle and the sharp flavours of the dressing.

The garnish
4–5 crisp lettuce leaves
1 garlic clove, finely chopped
1tbsp/15ml cooking oil
1 sprig coriander leaves, finely chopped

The yam
4tbsp/60ml vegetable stock (p. 85)
2oz/60g/^{2}/$_3$cup medium sized fresh button
mushrooms, sliced
4oz/120g dry clear vermicelli noodles, soaked in
water for 20 minutes until soft, then drained
2tbsp/30ml lemon juice
3tbsp/45ml light soy sauce
^{1}/$_2$tsp/2.5ml chili powder
1tsp/5ml sugar
2oz/60g/^{2}/$_3$cup pre-soaked dried black
fungus mushrooms
2oz/60g/^{2}/$_3$cup medium sized fresh button
mushrooms, sliced
2 shallots, finely sliced
1 spring onion/scallion, chopped
1 stalk celery with leaves, chopped
1 small carrot, finely chopped

Line a serving dish with lettuce and set aside. Fry the garlic in the oil until golden brown and set aside.

In a saucepan, heat the stock and add the fresh

(Back) Crudités; (left) green papaya salad; (right) mixed vegetable yam; (front) hot and sour vermicelli salad

mushrooms, cook momentarily, then add all the other yam ingredients and stir for approximately one minute until thoroughly mixed. Finally, add the garlic oil and mix, turn on to the lettuce and garnish with coriander.

GREEN PAPAYA SALAD

SOM TAM

This is another brilliant dish that is a product of poverty: the ingredients in Thailand are cheap and plentiful but the hot and spicy flavours elevate them out of the ordinary. You can find som tam all over the country, especially at wayside stops and garages where it is often served with a helping of sticky rice to make a cheap filling meal for travellers of modest means. In fact it is at roadside stalls that the dish always tastes best – it is never as good fancifully presented in a classy restaurant. If you go to Thailand be sure to try it at a bus stop or petrol station. It is the vegetarian's best standby, an emergency meal at any time of day in any corner of the country. If the Thai chili level looks too high you can always gesture with your hands to show you want less.

4oz/120g/½green papaya
1 garlic clove
3 small red or green chilis
1tbsp/15ml roast peanuts
1oz/30g/3–4 long beans chopped into 1inch/2.5cm
lengths (French beans may be substituted)
2tbsp/30ml lemon juice
3tbsp/45ml light soy sauce
1tsp/5ml sugar
1 medium tomato, chopped into segments
2 large leaves Chinese cabbage

Peel the outer skin from the green papaya and finely shred the flesh on a cheese grater or chop very finely into long thin shreds. Set aside. In a mortar, lightly pound the garlic, add the chilis and lightly pound again, add the peanuts and lightly pound while occasionally stirring with a spoon to prevent the resulting paste from thickening. Add the long beans and slightly bruise them. Add the shredded papaya, lightly pound and stir until all the ingredients are blended together. Add the lemon juice, soy sauce and sugar and stir into the mixture. Finally add the tomato, stirring once. Arrange the Chinese cabbage leaves on a serving dish and turn the yam on to them. Diners should tear off a section of cabbage leaf to use as a scoop for the yam, the two being eaten together. This dish is especially good with sticky rice (p. 50).

Green Papaya Salad
Take 1 large green papaya and peel with a knife.

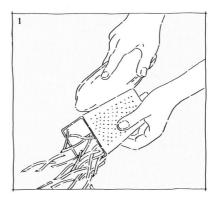

2 . . .give long shreds (using large holes of grater).

COOKED VEGETABLE YAM

YAM PAK DOM

1 garlic clove
2 shallots
1 large dried red chili
1tbsp/15ml sesame seeds
1oz/30g/3–4 long beans chopped into 1inch/2.5cm
lengths
1oz/30g/^{1}/$_4$cup purple aubergine/eggplant, coarsely
chopped
1oz/30g/about 4 leaves morning glory, coarsely
chopped
1oz/30g/^{1}/$_3$ cup bamboo shoots, coarsely chopped
1oz/30g/^{1}/$_3$ cup beansprouts
1tsp/5ml sugar
3tbsp/45ml light soy sauce
2tbsp/30ml lemon juice

To garnish
1 spring onion/scallion, finely chopped
coriander leaves

Put the garlic, shallots and dried chili under a hot grill/
broiler until just soft and there is a pleasant aroma of
burning. Transfer to a mortar, pound to a paste and set
aside.

Dry fry the sesame seeds until golden brown and set
aside.

Bring a pan of water to the boil and plunge the vegetables in it in the order listed until barely blanched and
still al dente. Drain, place in a large bowl, add the paste
to the warm vegetables and stir, add the sugar, soy and
lemon juice and stir thoroughly. Add the sesame seeds
and stir once. Garnish with the spring onion and
coriander and serve.

WING BEAN SALAD

YAM TUA PROO

8oz/230g/1 bundle wing beans, cut diagonally into
^{1}/$_8$inch/2mm slices
2tbsp/30ml coconut cream (p. 152)
2tbsp/30ml oil
3 garlic cloves, finely chopped
3 shallots, finely sliced
1tsp/5ml crushed dried red chili
1 ^{1}/$_2$tbsp/22.5ml Nam Prik Pow sauce (p. 140)
2tbsp/30ml ground roast peanuts
2tbsp/30ml lemon juice
2tbsp/30ml light soy sauce
1tsp/5ml sugar
2tbsp/30ml vegetable stock (p. 85)

Bring a pan of water to the boil. Put the beans in a wire
sieve, dip into the water for a few seconds to blanch,
then set aside. Gently heat the coconut cream in a
small pan until it thickens slightly, stirring from time to
time. In a small frying pan/skillet, heat the oil, add the
garlic and fry until golden brown and crisp. Remove the
garlic, drain and set aside. Add the shallot to the oil and
fry until golden brown and crisp. Remove and set aside.
Next, briefly fry the crushed dried chili, remove and set
aside. In a bowl mix the Nam Prik Pow with the ground
peanuts, lemon juice, light soy sauce, sugar and stock.
Add the fried garlic, shallots and dried chili. Mix
thoroughly. Add the beans and mix in gently until all
the ingredients are thoroughly blended. Turn on to a
serving dish and spoon the thickened coconut cream
over the top.

MANGO YAM

YAM MAMUANG

The difficulty with this dish is to find unripe green mangoes. Once found, it is delightfully easy to make. The chestnuts used here are the same as chestnuts found in the West and should not be confused with the water chestnuts that many people automatically associate with oriental food. In fact, chestnuts are commonly available all over Thailand, though given their abundance in the south of the country they may have originated in Malaysia.

4oz/120g/1 small whole green mango (do not peel), grated or finely chopped (like the green papaya, p. 53)
3 small fresh red or green chilis, finely chopped
3 shallots, finely chopped
1tsp/5ml sugar
1 garlic clove, finely chopped
2tbsp/30ml lemon juice
3tbsp/45ml light soy sauce
2tbsp/30ml whole roasted chestnuts

Briefly soak the grated or chopped mango in cold water to remove any syrup. Drain and put in a large bowl with all the other ingredients. Stir well and serve.

Mango yam

AUBERGINE YAM

YAM MAKUA

Ideally, track down the long thin pinkish aubergines, though they are difficult to find outside Asia. If this proves impossible then the more common bulbous purple/black variety must do.

2–3 long pinkish aubergines (p. 56) or 1–2 large
purple/black variety depending on size
3 shallots
2 garlic cloves
2 large fresh red chilis
2tbsp/30ml light soy sauce
1tsp/5ml sugar
2tbsp/30ml lemon juice
1tbsp/15ml sesame seeds dry 'roasted' in a frying
pan/skillet

To garnish
10 mint leaves

Grill/broil the aubergine until the skin can be pulled away easily. Try not to burn the flesh and cut away any that is accidentally charred. Slice the flesh into $^1/_2$ inch/1.25cm thick wheels and set aside.

Grill/broil the shallots, garlic and chillies until cooked but not charred. Place in a mortar and pound to a rough paste.

Put the sliced aubergine in a bowl with the paste and stir to coat. Add the light soy sauce, sugar, lemon juice and sesame seeds and stir together. Turn on to a serving dish and garnish with mint leaves.

AUBERGINE/EGGPLANT

Four varieties of aubergine are used in this book, though only the first is readily available.

● The large purple/black aubergine familiar in the West. If this is used as a substitute for the others care should be taken to adjust cooking times down to allow for its softer texture.

● The long thin pink-skinned aubergine. These can sometimes be found in the West and as they are firmer than the darker variety they make a better substitute for the smaller varieties.

● The small, round, green aubergine (about 1inch/2.5cm in diameter). Sometimes available in Asian stores in major cities.

● The pea aubergine, a green aubergine slightly larger than a garden pea. Sometimes available in Asian stores in major cities.

LONG BEAN SALAD

YAM TUA FAK YOW

1 garlic clove
3 small red or green chilis
4oz/120g/1 bundle long beans (use French beans
if unavailable)
2tbsp/30ml light soy sauce
2tbsp/30ml lemon juice
1tsp/5ml sugar
1 medium tomato, roughly sliced
1tbsp/15ml crushed roast peanuts
4 or 5 lettuce leaves (or Chinese cabbage etc.)

In a mortar, pound the garlic and the chili until well crushed. Add the long beans and lightly pound until slightly broken. Add the soy sauce, lemon juice and sugar, stirring well. Add the tomato, stir quickly; add the crushed peanuts, stir quickly. Arrange the salad leaves on a serving dish and turn the yam mixture on to them. Eat with fingers using the leaves as scoops.

BEANSPROUT YAM

YAM TUA NGOK

1tbsp/15ml oil
1 garlic clove, finely chopped
4oz/120g/1 1/4 cups beansprouts
1tbsp/15ml white vinegar
2tbsp/30ml light soy sauce
1 large red chili, finely sliced into rings
1/2 tsp/2.5ml sugar
1/2 tsp/2.5ml chili powder
2tbsp/30ml ground roast peanuts

To garnish
1 spring onion/scallion, finely chopped
coriander leaves

Fill a medium sized pan with water and bring to the boil. Meanwhile, heat the oil, fry the garlic until crispy, remove, drain and set aside.

When the water boils dip in the beansprouts for 2–3 seconds to blanch them. Strain and turn into a bowl, add the other ingredients and toss. Sprinkle the crispy garlic over the mixture and garnish with the spring onion and coriander.

BEANCURD SALAD

YAM TAO HOU

1tbsp/30ml kow kua rice grains (see below)
3 shallots, finely chopped
1 garlic clove, finely chopped
1tbsp/15ml finely chopped galangal
10oz/300g/2 1/2 cups soft white beancurd
oil for deep-frying
2tbsp/30ml light soy sauce
1tsp/5ml sugar
2tbsp/30ml lemon juice
1 tsp/5ml chili powder
1 spring onion/scallion, finely chopped into rings
5 lettuce leaves

To garnish
10 mint leaves

To make the kow kua: dry fry the rice grains in a small pan without oil for 4–5 minutes until pale brown. In a mortar, pound the grains into a coarse powder.

Dry-fry the shallots, garlic and galangal until the garlic is soft and the ensemble gives off a pleasant aroma of burning – without actually burning. Place in a mortar, pound to a paste and set aside.

Slice the beancurd into 16 squares per block. Deep-fry until the outside is golden brown while the interior remains white. Turn into a bowl, add the paste from the mortar and stir well. Add the light soy sauce, sugar, lemon juice, chili powder, kow kua and spring onion. Stir well, turn on to the lettuce leaves and garnish with mint.

BAMBOO SHOOT SALAD

YAM NORMAI

4oz/120g/1 ¼ cups bamboo shoots
2 shallots
1 garlic clove
1tsp/5ml uncooked rice grains
1tsp/5ml sesame seeds
4tbsp/60ml vegetable stock (p. 85)
2tbsp/30ml lemon juice
3tbsp/45ml light soy sauce
1tsp/5ml sugar
1tsp/5ml chili powder
10 mint leaves
1 spring onion/scallion, finely chopped
2 large Chinese cabbage leaves
2 long beans, chopped into 4inch/10cm lengths

With a knife, scrape the pieces of bamboo shoot to make long matchstick gratings and set aside.

Grill/broil the shallots and garlic until they are soft and give off a pleasant slightly burnt aroma – without actually burning. Place in a mortar and pound together, then set aside.

Place the grains of rice and the sesame seeds in a dry frying pan/skillet and heat until golden. Set aside.

Put the stock into a saucepan and bring to the boil.

Add the bamboo shoot gratings, the pounded shallot and garlic, lemon juice, soy sauce, sugar and chili powder and stir well. Remove from the heat. Add the 'roasted' rice and sesame seeds, the mint leaves and spring onion, stirring briefly. Arrange the Chinese cabbage leaves and the long beans around the edge of a serving dish, turn the mixture into the centre and serve.

CUCUMBER SALAD

YAM TANG GWA

4oz/120g/about ⅓ cucumber
1 garlic clove
2 small red or green chilis
2tbsp/30ml lemon juice
3tbsp/45ml light soy sauce
1tsp/5ml sugar
1 medium sized tomato, chopped into segments
1tbsp/15ml ground roast peanuts

Either chop the cucumber lengthwise into very fine matchsticks or grate it with long strokes on the large blade of a cheese grater, and place in a bowl. In a mortar, pound together the garlic and chilis and add to the cucumber. Mix in the lemon juice, soy, sugar and tomato. Finally add the ground peanuts, turn once and serve.

Cucumber salad and bamboo shoot salad

STARTERS AND SNACKS

THE WEEKEND MARKET

When I was young, my friends and I would look forward all week to the famous Sunday Market which was held on the Sanam Luang or Field of Kings, next to the Grand Palace by the Chao Phya river in central Bangkok. The market was a fascinating riot of colour where everything from fruit to shirts could be found. Half the city seemed to crowd into the narrow rows of covered stalls, everyone looking for a bargain. That was the problem, the Sanam Luang was too small for so popular a meeting place and several years ago what has now become the Weekend Market was moved to Paholyotin Road further out of town. It has grown beyond belief with stalls selling locally made Gucci bags, antiques, army surplus equipment, videos, snakes . . . if you want it you'll find it, provided you can stand the heat under the canvas awnings and in the airless corridors between the stalls.

The Chatuchak Weekend Market is one of the world's great sights and a must for vegetarians, for just across the road from the main food market is a long open pavilion run by the Bangkok Vegetarian Society. The society is headed by the present Governor of

Festivities in honour of Thailand's reigning dynasty with the spires of the Grand Palace in the background

Market woman making spring roll sheets

Bangkok, General Chamlong Srimuang, an extraordinary political reformer who has pledged himself to provide the capital with a corruption-free administration. The son of a poor family, the General is determined to do something for the city's under-class, those who live in the squalid slums out of sight of most tourists. General Chamlong's beliefs encompass a whole range of ideas concerned with spiritual renewal of which vegetarianism is one, and he and his wife are directly involved in the running of the vegetarian restaurant at the Weekend Market. Quite simply, the food offered there is delicious and the range of dishes astonishing. Indeed the sheer variety is so tempting that the first-time visitor usualiy forgoes a single large course so as to sample as many small starters as possible.

One of the advantages of Thai cookery is that you can eat quite lightly if you wish. There has always been a tradition of serving light afternoon snacks in Thai homes and it is possible to compose a meal entirely of these small delicious dishes. There is, however, no tradition of the first course or starter in Thai cuisine; though it was usual for some of the spicier dishes such as yams to be brought out as soon as they were prepared, so that the waiting diners could nibble at them while enjoying a pre-meal drink.

Two things have now nudged some of these dishes into a separate category of starters. Firstly there was the need to adapt Thai cookery for the tourists who visit my country and for those Thai restaurants in countries where diners like a first, lighter course before the main meal. Secondly there was the demand for food that can be served at parties and receptions. This chapter brings together some of those dishes. If you wish to eat in the traditional way, simply think of these dishes as part of the main meal.

If you intend to use these recipes for parties you will need to increase the quantities given in relation to the numbers of guests you expect.

I hope that when you next visit Bangkok you will also find the time to go out to what is more properly called the Chatuchak Weekend Market. You'll have to learn to bargain, amiably but forcefully, but that's all part of the fun. You should also visit the sight of the old Sunday Market, for now that it is no longer covered in stalls the Sanam Luang hosts a variety of Sunday entertainments. In March and April there are kite duels with two teams, each determined to bring down the kites of their opponents. There is an annual royal ploughing ceremony and many religious ceremonies, the most spectacular being a rare royal cremation. When I was last in Bangkok there was a celebration of the nine reigns of the present dynasty with models representing a noteworthy building associated with each king. In addition there were the inevitable food stalls and contests of takraw – Thai kick ball – and even a pop concert. Thai pop music is a world of its own, homegrown

Hit Parade stars are adored by their screaming fans.

The newcomer to Bangkok naturally heads first for the main sights: the Emerald Buddha, the Grand Palace, The Temple of the Dawn, but if you can, explore the older parts of the city near the river, where you can meet at every turn an ancient wooden shop with carved shutters, an unusual bridge over a klong, or catch a glimpse of a temple set back from the street. Then take the river bus and see some of the rare remaining sights of old Siam: wooden houses built right out into the water, Portuguese mission churches, the earliest Western embassies in white stucco with their formal waterside gardens. It is all a wonderful change from the hectic, motor-car clogged modern metropolis that most of the working inhabitants have to suffer.

'Once Upon a Time' – a restaurant in one of the few surviving houses in central Bangkok. (Left) Wing bean salad; (right) crispy rice with coconut and mushroom sauce

STEAMED STUFFED WON TON

KANOM JEEP Ⓔ

Won ton pastry leaves are made from egg and flour and are sold ready-made in $3\frac{1}{4}$inch/8cm squares. They can be wrapped and stored in a refrigerator for 4–5 days.

1 egg
15 black peppercorns
2 coriander roots, roughly chopped
2tbsp/30ml oil
2 small garlic cloves, finely chopped
4oz/120g/1$\frac{1}{4}$cups bamboo shoots, finely diced
4oz/120g/1$\frac{1}{4}$cups water chestnuts, finely diced
4oz/120g/1 large onion, finely diced
2tsp/10ml plain flour
2tbsp/30ml light soy sauce
1tsp/5ml sugar
20 sheets won ton pastry

To garnish
lettuce and coriander leaves

Hardboil the egg, remove the yolk, finely chop and set aside. Take the white, finely chop and set aside.

In a mortar, pound the peppercorns and coriander roots until a paste forms and set aside.

In a wok or frying pan/skillet heat the oil, fry the garlic golden brown and set aside with the oil.

In a bowl, mix the bamboo shoots, water chestnuts, onion, the paste, the flour, soy sauce, sugar and egg white, stirring well until a firm mixture is formed.

Separate the won ton leaves. At the centre of each, place a nugget of filling. Gather up the edges of the pastry square and crimp together to form a tiny 'money bag'. Put a little egg yolk in the mouth of each bag. Arrange the bags in a steamer and steam for 15 minutes. Just before serving drip a little garlic oil on to each bag then serve with Sour Soy Sauce, below.

Sour Soy Sauce
3tbsp/45ml light soy sauce
1tbsp/15ml white vinegar
1tsp/5ml sugar
3 small red or green chilis, finely chopped

Place all the ingredients in a small serving bowl, stir and serve.

STEAMED STUFFED SAGO

SA KU

8oz/230g/1 cup uncooked sago (p. 14)
4tbsp/60ml hot water
1tsp/5ml coarsely chopped garlic
1tsp/5ml roughly chopped coriander root
1tsp/5ml whole black peppercorns
2tbsp/30ml oil
2oz/60g/$\frac{1}{4}$ cup chi po, preserved turnip, finely chopped
2oz/60g/$\frac{1}{3}$ cup ground roast peanuts
2tsp/10ml sugar

To garnish
lettuce leaves
fresh coriander
5 small red chilis
garlic oil (1tsp/5ml finely chopped garlic,
fried golden brown in 1tbsp/15ml oil)

Knead the sago in the hot water to make a thick dough and set aside.

In a mortar, pound together the garlic, coriander root and peppercorns to form a paste. In a wok or frying pan/skillet, heat the oil, add the paste and fry very briefly, stirring, then add the preserved turnip, ground peanuts and sugar, stir well and set aside.

With dampened hands, take a ball of the sago dough

Steamed stuffed sago – noble families in nineteenth-century Siam had a passion for Victorian cut-glass

(roughly 1tsp/5ml) and on the wet palm of one hand flatten it into a patty. Place $^{1}/_{2}$ tsp/2.5ml of the fried mixture at the centre of the patty and mould it back into a ball. Place all the stuffed sago balls in a steamer over boiling water for about 20 minutes, until the pearly white sago grains have become transparent and jelly-like. The time this takes will depend on the thickness of the sago dough you have made.

Arrange the lettuce on a serving dish and place the steamed sago balls at the centre of the dish. Decorate with a cluster of coriander leaves and red chilis. Just before serving, sprinkle with the garlic oil. The sago balls should be eaten with a scoop of lettuce and a nibble of coriander and chili.

MUSHROOM LAAB

LAAB HET

8oz/230g/2²/₃ cups fresh button mushrooms,
finely diced
2tbsp/30ml light soy sauce
2tbsp/30ml lemon juice
1tsp/5ml sugar
1tsp/5ml chili powder
1tsp/5ml lemon grass, finely chopped
1tsp/5ml galangal, finely chopped
1tsp/5ml kaffir lime leaf, finely chopped
2tsp/10ml khao kua (p. 57)
1 spring onion/scallion, finely chopped into rings
10 mint leaves
2 large Chinese cabbage leaves
2 long beans chopped into 4inch/10cm lengths

Dip the diced mushrooms in boiling water to blanch. Remove and drain. Place in a large mixing bowl and add all the ingredients down to and including the mint leaves, stirring well. Arrange the cabbage leaves on a serving dish and turn the mixture on to them. Arrange the long beans at one edge of the dish and serve. Diners should break off pieces of cabbage to scoop up the laab and eat with a piece of bean.

MUSHROOM SATAY

SATAY HET HOM

For this recipe you will need to buy satay sticks from an Asian store. These are thin slivers of wood painted at one end, like an outsize toothpick, sold in packets. There are outsize cocktail sticks that would do as an alternative.

8oz/230g/2²/₃ cups pre-soaked dried Chinese
mushrooms

Taking each mushroom as a rough circle cut towards the centre in a sprial to make one long strip as if peeling an apple in one go. Set aside.

The marinade
1tsp/5ml finely chopped galangal
1tsp/5ml finely chopped lemon grass
1tsp/5ml finely chopped kaffir lime leaf
2 coriander roots
4 small garlic cloves, coarsely chopped
¹/₂tsp/2.5ml ground black pepper
2tbsp/30ml curry powder
1tbsp/30ml light soy sauce
2tbsp/30ml sugar
1tsp/5ml powdered coriander seeds
1tsp/5ml ground cumin
1tsp/5ml salt
2tbsp/30ml oil
4fl oz/120ml/¹/₂cup coconut milk

In a mortar pound together the galangal, lemon grass, lime leaf, coriander roots and garlic to form a paste. Place this in a mixing bowl and stir in all the other ingredients, mixing well. Place all the mushroom strips in this marinade and leave for at least 30 minutes.

The peanut sauce
1tbsp/15ml oil
1tbsp/15ml red curry paste (p. 105)
8fl oz/240ml/1cup coconut milk
2tbsp/30ml sugar
¹/₄tsp/1.25ml salt
1tbsp/15ml lemon juice
3tbsp/45ml ground roast peanuts

In a wok or frying pan/skillet, heat the oil, add the curry paste and fry briefly until it blends with the oil. Add the coconut milk, lower the heat and stir well until a rich red colour appears. Add the remaining ingredients, stirring constantly until a thick sauce is formed, and set aside.

Take the mushroom strips from the marinade and thread each one on to a satay stick. Grill/broil until cooked through. Serve with the peanut sauce (p. 66) and fresh cucumber pickle (p. 69). Little triangles of toast may also be served for those who wish to mop up more sauce.

FRIED BEANCURD WITH SWEET NUT SAUCE

TAO HOU TOD

16oz/480g/4cups ready-fried beancurd
oil for deep frying
5tbsp/75ml white vinegar
4tbsp/60ml sugar
1tsp/5ml salt
$^1/_2$tsp/2.5ml chili powder
2tbsp/30ml ground roast peanuts

To garnish
coriander leaves

Slice the beancurd cubes in half diagonally and deep-fry the eight triangles until the white side is golden brown. Drain and arrange on a serving dish and set aside.

In a saucepan heat the vinegar, sugar and salt until the mixture thickens. Remove from the heat and add the chili powder and ground peanuts, stirring well until all the ingredients are thoroughly mixed. Turn into a serving bowl, garnish with coriander leaves and serve with the beancurd.

GRILLED SPICY MUSHROOMS

HET NAM TOK

8oz/230g/2$^2/_3$cups large flat mushrooms, stems
removed, wiped with a damp cloth
2tbsp/30ml light soy sauce
2tbsp/30ml lemon juice
2tbsp/30ml vegetable stock (p. 85)
$^1/_2$tsp/2.5ml chili powder
$^1/_2$tsp/2.5ml sugar
2 small shallots, finely chopped into rounds
1 medium spring onion/scallion, finely chopped
into rings
1tsp/5ml rice, dry-fried and ground
1 whole coriander cluster (stems and leaves but
without the root), finely chopped
lettuce leaves
10 mint leaves, finely chopped
3 long beans, chopped into 3inch/7.5cm lengths

Grill/broil the mushrooms briefly, turning once until the skin is slightly cooked and they are warmed through, but still firm. Slice crossways into $^1/_8$inch/2mm strips. Place in a pan and gently heat while adding all the ingredients down to and including the spring onion rings, stirring well. Remove from the heat, add the ground rice, coriander and mint, stir well and serve on a bed of lettuce, mint leaves and long beans.

FRIED WON TON

GEEOW TOD

1tsp/5ml roughly chopped garlic
1tsp/5ml roughly chopped coriander root
1tsp/5ml whole black peppercorns
2tbsp/30ml oil
2tbsp/30ml dried moong beans, soaked for 30
minutes then drained
¹/₂tsp/2.5ml salt
¹/₂tsp/2.5ml sugar
20 sheets won ton pastry
oil for deep frying

In a mortar pound the garlic, coriander root and peppercorns to form a paste and set aside.

Heat the oil in a wok or frying pan/skillet, add the paste and stir briefly. Drain the moong beans and stir into the oil. Add the salt and sugar and stir well. Place a nugget of this filling at the centre of each won ton pastry square. Fold the square in half diagonally to make a triangle. Use a little water to seal the sides. Deep-fry the stuffed won ton until golden brown, drain and serve with the following sauces.

Sweet and hot sauces
6tbsp/90ml rice vinegar
4tbsp/60ml sugar
¹/₂tsp/2.5ml salt
1 small red chili, finely chopped
1 small green chili, finely chopped

Gently heat the vinegar, sugar and salt until the sugar dissolves. Allow to cool and pour into two small serving bowls. Stir the chopped chilis into one of them.

In the Vegetarian Pavilion at the Chatuchak Weekend Market –
(front) mushroom laab (p. 66); (back left) fried won ton; (back
right) fried beancurd with sweet nut sauce (p. 67)

FRIED BREAD AND YELLOW BEAN PASTE

KANOM BANG NA TOOAH Ⓔ

Well before beginning this recipe you should prepare the bread as it must not be too fresh. Leave some slices of bread unwrapped for a day so that they will dry a little, otherwise you will have to quick-dry them in a warm oven.

1tsp/5ml roughly chopped garlic
1tsp/5ml whole black peppercorns
1tsp/5ml roughly chopped coriander root
4fl oz/120ml/$^1/_2$cup dried moong beans, soaked for
30 minutes then drained
1 egg, whisked
1tbsp/5ml light soy sauce
$^1/_2$tsp/2.5ml sugar
36 1inch/2.5cm bread squares
coriander leaves
oil for deep frying

In a mortar, pound together the garlic, peppercorns and coriander root to form a paste. Add the drained moong beans and pound together, add half the whisked egg, the soy sauce and sugar and stir well to form a thick paste. Place a nugget of the paste on each bread square, pressing it down so that it sticks. Coat with whisked egg and decorate with a coriander leaf. Deep-fry until golden brown and serve with fresh cucumber pickle, A jad, below.

Fresh Cucumber Pickle
4tbsp/60ml rice vinegar
2tsp/10ml sugar
$^1/_2$tsp/2.5ml salt
1oz/30g/1 small chunk cucumber, finely chopped
2 small shallots, finely chopped
1 small carrot, finely chopped
1 small red or green chili, finely chopped

Mix all the ingredients in a small bowl, stirring well until thoroughly mixed and serve.

FRIED TARO

POOAK TOD Ⓔ

1 egg
3tbs/45ml coconut milk
3tbs/45ml plain flour
$^1/_2$tsp/2.5ml salt
1tbs/15ml sugar
1tbs/15ml sesame seeds
10oz/300g/1$^2/_3$ taro peeled and chopped into large
'chips' (bigger than French fries)
Oil for deep frying

In a large mixing bowl, mix together the egg, coconut milk, flour, salt, sugar and sesame seeds, stirring well. Place the taro chips in the mixture, turning until well coated. Heat the oil and deep fry the battered chips until golden brown, drain and place on a serving dish.

4tbs/60ml white vinegar
3tbs/45ml sugar
$^1/_2$tsp/2.5ml salt
2oz/60g/1 chunk cucumber, thinly sliced
2oz/60g/2 carrots, thinly sliced
3 small red shallots, chopped into thin rings
2 small red or green chilis, finely chopped
1tbs/15ml ground roast peanuts

To garnish
coriander leaves

In a saucepan, gently heat the vinegar, sugar and salt until the sugar dissolves. Allow to cool then pour into a serving bowl. Mix in all the remaining ingredients, garnish with coriander leaves and serve with taro chips.

GOLDEN FLOWERS

GRATONG TONG Ⓔ

There is a Thai implement for making the batter cases called 'golden flowers' or 'golden baskets' but you can use a small ladle with a bowl about 2 inches/5cm in diameter.

The flowers
8oz/230g/2cups flour
½tsp/2.5ml salt
1 egg
8fl oz/250ml/1cup water
oil for deep-frying

In a bowl, mix the flour and salt, break in the egg and mix. Gradually add the water, stirring constantly until there is a thick creamy batter. Allow to rest for an hour. Heat the oil, dip the ladle bowl into the hot oil, remove and shake then dip into the batter to coat the outer surface. Return to the oil. After 20 seconds the case should be cooked enough to float free. Continue to fry until golden brown. Remove, drain and set aside.

The filling
2tbsp/30ml oil
1tsp/5ml finely chopped garlic
3oz/90g/²⁄₃cup sweetcorn off the cob
3oz/90g/1–2 carrots, finely diced
3oz/90g/1 large onion, finely chopped
3oz/90g/1 large potato, finely diced
1tbsp/15ml light soy sauce
½tsp/2.5ml salt
½tsp/2.5ml sugar
1tsp/5ml curry powder
½tsp/2.5ml ground turmeric
½tsp/2.5ml ground white pepper

To garnish
coriander leaves

In a wok or frying pan/skillet, heat the oil, fry the garlic until golden brown, then add each vegetable in turn, stirring constantly. Stir-fry until the potato is almost cooked, then add all the remaining ingredients and mix thoroughly. Remove from the heat, allow to cool, then fill the batter cases with the mixture. Garnish each with a coriander leaf and serve.

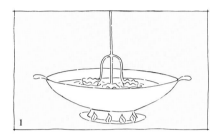

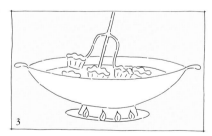

Golden Flowers
For this you need a flower spoon or a small ladle spoon.

1 Dip a fluted spoon on a stem or long-handled ladle spoon into a wok or pan of hot oil.
2 Then dip it into the batter to coat it.
3 Dip immediately into hot oil. Hold the spoon, dipping it slightly up and down to free the batter flower shell so it will float away.

Leave the flowers until golden brown.

SPRING ROLLS

PO PEA TOD

The filling
4oz/120g soaked wun sen noodles, finely chopped
2oz/60g/²/₃cup pre-soaked dried black fungus
mushrooms, finely chopped
2oz/60g/¹/₂cup beansprouts
2oz/60g/1–2 carrots, finely diced
1tsp/2.5ml finely chopped garlic
1tbsp/15ml light soy sauce
¹/₂tsp/12.5ml sugar
¹/₂tsp/2.5ml ground white pepper

Place all the ingredients in a large mixing bowl and stir
well. Set aside.

The rolls
1tbsp/30ml cornflour/cornstarch
6 large spring roll sheets, quartered
oil for deep frying
raw salad (lettuce, mint leaves, red basil leaves,
sliced cucumber etc.)

Mix the flour with a little water to make a paste and set
aside. Place a little of the filling on each quartered
spring roll sheet, fold in two opposite corners then roll
across them into a plump cigarette as illustrated. Use a
little of the paste to seal. Heat the oil and deep-fry the
rolls until golden brown, drain and serve with the salad
and the sweet sauce (see p. 72).

Spring Rolls

1 Using a square of spring roll sheet turn it to point towards you
(as a diamond). Place the mixture in the middle.
2 Begin to roll up the edge to cover the mixture.
3 When about half rolled up, bring in the two triangles at the
sides. Roll up once more.
4 This will leave a top flap (like an envelope). Cover this with egg
yolk (dab on with your finger) to seal the roll and fold up
completely.

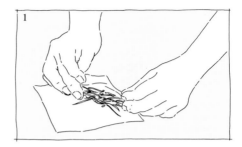

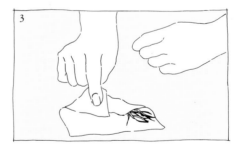

VEGETABLE SAUSAGE

HOY JAW

Beancurd sheets are the skin which forms on the surface of boiled soy milk as it cools. They are sold dried and should be soaked in a large flat dish of water for about 15 minutes before using.

1tbsp/15ml flour
2tbsp/30ml water
1tsp/5ml coarsely chopped garlic
1tsp/5ml coarsely chopped coriander root
1tsp/5ml whole black peppercorns
2tbsp/30ml oil
2oz/60g/about 1/3 taro, peeled and
coarsely chopped
2oz/60g/1–2 carrots, coarsely chopped
2oz/60g/1/2 cup water chestnuts, coarsely chopped
2oz/60g/1 stalk celery, coarsely chopped
2oz/60g/2/3 cup pre-soaked dried Chinese
mushrooms, coarsely chopped
2oz/60g/1/2 cup beansprouts, coarsely chopped
2tbsp/30ml light soy sauce
1tsp/5ml sugar
3 large beancurd sheets
oil for deep-frying

To garnish
lettuce and mint leaves

Mix the flour and water to form a paste and set aside. In a mortar pound together the garlic, coriander root and peppercorns to form a paste. Heat the oil and briefly fry the garlic paste, then add all the remaining ingredients down to and including the sugar, stirring constantly. Add the flour and water paste and stir to thicken. Remove from the heat and leave to cool.

Drain the beancurd sheets and spread out on a flat surface. Place a line of the cooled filling along one edge of each sheet and roll to form a long sausage. Place the 3 sausages in a steamer and steam for 15 minutes. Remove and leave to cool.

When ready to serve, deep-fry the sausages until golden brown, drain and slice into 1/4 inch/6mm rounds and serve on a bed of lettuce and mint leaves with Plum Sauce (p. 79).

DEEP-FRIED YELLOW BEAN PASTE

BAA YIR

4oz/120g/2/3 cup dried moong beans,
soaked in water
for 30 minutes and drained
1tbsp/15ml plain flour
2tsp/10ml red curry paste (p. 105)
1tbsp/15ml light soy sauce
1tsp/5ml sugar
2 kaffir lime leaves, rolled into a cigarette
and finely sliced into slivers
oil for deep-frying

In a mortar pound the drained moong beans to form a paste. Add the other ingredients in turn, stirring well. Pluck a small piece of the paste and form into a ball the size of a walnut. Do not mould too tightly. Deep-fry the balls until golden brown, drain and serve with the thick sweet sauce below.

The sauce
4tbsp/60ml sugar
6tbsp/90ml rice vinegar
1/2tsp/2.5ml salt

Gently heat the three ingredients until the sugar dissolves. Allow to cool before serving.

Deep-fried yellow bean paste

CRISPY RICE WITH COCONUT AND MUSHROOM SAUCE

KHAO TUNG NAA TANG

This dish is delicious, which makes it all the more surprising that it seems to be unknown outside Bangkok. My grandmother used to make it for us but since her death I had almost forgotten about it until a recent visit to a wonderful Bangkok restaurant called, appropriately, Once Upon A Time, where I found it on the menu. It was a true trip down memory lane – the restaurant is in one of the few surviving wooden houses in the centre of the city and is decorated with old bric-à-brac and Thai film posters from the Fifties, all jumbled up together.

The recipe here is really a clever way out of what is in effect a culinary accident! If you cook rice frequently you are bound to have an unlucky day when a thin layer sticks to the bottom of the pan. This is a way of turning the accident to advantage: after the usable rice has been removed from the pan the slightly burned layer is left to cool, then peeled off like a flat pancake. This is left to dry out further and then fried until golden brown and crispy. Naturally, a restaurant like Once Upon A Time cannot rely on accidents, so they have developed their own way of creating the Khao Tung, as the crispy rice is called.

Crispy Rice
20tbsp/300g/2 1/2 cups cold boiled rice
oil for deep frying

Take a ball of cold rice (about 2tbsp/30g) and press between the palms to form a pancake about ¼inch/6mm thick. This quantity should make around 10 pancakes.

Deep-fry the pancakes until golden brown and crispy, drain and set aside.

The sauce
1tsp/5ml roughly chopped garlic
1tsp/5ml roughly chopped coriander root
1tsp/5ml whole black peppercorns
2tbsp/30ml oil
2 small shallots, finely chopped
4oz/120g/1 1/3 cups straw mushrooms, finely chopped
8fl oz/240ml/1cup coconut milk
1tsp/5ml sugar
2tbsp/30ml light soy sauce
1tbsp/15ml tamarind juice (or 2tbsp/30ml lemon juice)
2tbsp/30ml ground roast peanuts
1 large red chili, finely diced

To garnish
coriander leaves

In a mortar, pound the garlic, coriander root and peppercorns to form a paste. Heat the oil and briefly fry the paste. Add the shallots, stir, add the mushrooms, stir, add the coconut milk and stir well. Stir in all the remaining ingredients mixing thoroughly. Turn into a serving bowl, garnish with coriander leaves and serve with the crispy rice 'biscuits'.

SPRING FLOWER LEAF CAKE

KANOM GUI CHI

The dough
5oz/150g/1 1/4 cups rice flour
4oz/120g/1 1/4 cups tapioca flour
6tbsp/90ml oil
16fl oz/480ml/2cups water
1/2 tsp/2.5ml salt

Knead all the ingredients together to make a dough and set aside.

The filling
3tbsp/45ml oil
1tsp/5ml finely chopped garlic
8oz/230g/1 bundle gui chi, spring flower leaves, finely chopped
1tsp/5ml ground white pepper
2tbsp/30ml light soy sauce
$1/2$tsp/2.5ml salt
1tsp/5ml sugar

Heat the oil in a frying pan/skillet and fry the garlic until golden brown, then add the other ingredients, stirring constantly, and set aside.

Divide the dough into five, take one piece, form into a ball, then press into a flat patty. Place 1tbsp/15ml of the filling in the centre, fold the dough over and press into a flat patty again. Repeat with the remaining dough. Place the five patties in a steamer over boiling water for 7 minutes. You can eat them steamed as they are or let them cool then deep-fry in oil until golden. In both cases serve with the following sauce.

The sauce
2tbsp/30ml light soy sauce
2tbsp/30ml dark soy sauce
2tbsp/30ml white vinegar
2 large fresh red chilis, finely sliced into rings
1tsp/5ml sugar

Mix the ingredients together in a small bowl and serve.

SPICY RICE AND NOODLE
NAM SOT

5 small dried red chilis
oil for deep-frying
4oz/120g/1 cup ready-fried beancurd, finely chopped
4oz/120g/1cup boiled rice
4oz/120g soaked sen lek noodles, chopped into 1inch/2.5cm lengths
3 small shallots, finely chopped
2 inches/5cm piece ginger root, cut into fine matchsticks
2tbsp/30ml light soy sauce
3tbsp/45ml lemon juice
1tsp/5ml sugar
2oz/60g/$1/3$cup whole roast peanuts
2 medium spring onions/scallions, finely chopped into rings

To garnish
lettuce leaves
coriander leaves

Heat the oil and deep-fry the chilis until swollen, remove, chop finely and set aside. Deep-fry the chopped beancurd until the white sides are golden brown, drain and set aside. Tightly mould the rice into balls roughly 1inch/2.5cm in diameter and deep-fry until golden brown, then drain. With your fingers, break the balls into fragments into a mixing bowl – some will be hard and brown, and some soft and white.

Bring a pan of water to the boil, briefly dip the noodles then plunge into cold water to arrest the cooking. Put the cold noodles into the bowl with the broken rice. Add the deep-fried chilis and beancurd, add all the remaining ingredients and stir well. Turn on to a bed of lettuce leaves and garnish with coriander.

VEGETABLE SAMOSAS

SA MO SA

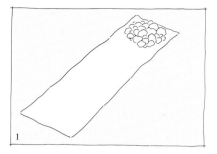

The filling
1tsp/5ml roughly chopped garlic
1tsp/5ml roughly chopped coriander root
1tsp/5ml whole black peppercorns
2tbsp/30ml oil
3oz/90g/1 sweet potato, finely diced
3oz/90g/1 large onion, finely diced
3oz/90g/2 carrots, finely diced
3oz/90g/²⁄₃ cup boiled sweetcorn (off the cob)
¹⁄₂tsp/2.5ml salt
1tsp/5ml curry powder
1tbsp/15ml light soy sauce
1tsp/5ml sugar

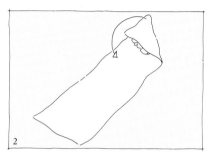

In a mortar pound together the garlic, coriander root and peppercorns to form a paste. Heat the oil, briefly fry the paste then add the other ingredients in turn, stirring constantly. Set aside.

The samosas
4 large spring roll sheets
1tbsp/30ml cornflour/cornstarch, mixed with hot water to make a thick paste
oil for deep frying

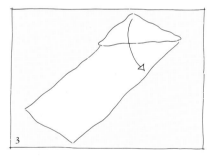

Cut the spring roll sheets into three long strips. Place a large nugget of the paste on each strip and fold as illustrated, using the flour and water paste to seal. Heat the oil and deep-fry the samosas until golden brown, drain and serve with fresh cucumber pickle (p. 69).

Samosa

1 Cut a large oblong strip (about 1×5in) from a large spring roll sheet. Put a dab of mixture on the edge nearest you.
2 Fold up an edge diagonally to form a triangle.
3 Fold up each edge diagonally until you have practically reached the end and dab a piece of egg yolk on the final corner.
4 Fold over to seal.

GOLD BAGS

TUNG TONG

1tsp/5ml coarsely chopped garlic
1tsp/5ml coarsely chopped coriander root
1tsp/5ml whole black peppercorns
8oz/230g/1 ½ cups mashed boiled potato
6oz/180g/1 ½ cups water chestnuts, finely diced
2tbsp/30ml ground roast peanuts
1tbsp/15ml light soy sauce
½ tsp/2.5ml salt
½ tsp/2.5ml sugar
3 large spring roll sheets, quartered
1tbsp/30ml cornflour/cornstarch, mixed with hot
water to make a thick paste
oil for deep-frying

In a mortar, pound the garlic, coriander root and pep-percorns to form a paste. In a bowl mix the paste with all the other ingredients down to and including the sugar. Stir thoroughly. Place a nugget of this mixture on each quartered spring roll sheet and fold as illustrated using the flour and water paste to seal. Deep-fry until golden brown, drain and serve with the sweet and hot sauce (see p. 72).

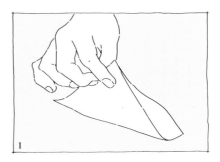

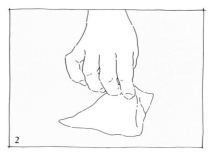

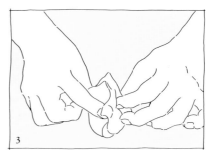

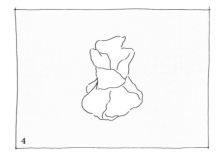

Gold Bag

Use the same size square of spring roll sheet as for a spring roll and put mixture in centre.
1 Bring opposite sides up to form a triangle.
2 Then gather in the other two corners to form a pouch.
3 Put a little egg yolk (with your finger) in the gathers of the pouch to hold it together.
4 Fluff out the gathers to make it look like a money bag.

SWEETCORN CAKES

TOD MAN KHAO POHD

12oz/340g/2²/₃cups raw sweetcorn, off the cob
1tbsp/15ml curry powder
2tbsp/30ml rice flour
3tbsp/45ml wheat flour
¹/₂tsp/2.5ml salt
2tbsp/30ml light soy sauce
oil for deep-frying

In a bowl, mix together all the ingredients, except the oil, stirring well to make a thick dough. Heat the oil. Using a spoon form the dough into small cakes and slide into the hot oil. Deep-fry until golden brown, drain, allow to cool and serve with Fresh Cucumber Pickle (p. 69).

Sweetcorn cakes

MUSHROOM BALLS

LOOK CHIN HET Ⓔ

5oz/145g/1 ¹/₄cups flour
6tbsp/90ml water
¹/₂tsp/2.5ml salt
¹/₂tsp/2.5ml ground white pepper
1tsp/5ml sesame seeds
1 egg
8oz/230g/2²/₃cups fresh button mushrooms, left
whole
oil for deep-frying

In a bowl mix together the flour, water, salt, pepper and sesame seeds. Break the egg into the mixture and stir well to make a batter. Set aside.

Blanch the mushrooms in boiling water then immediately plunge them into cold water to arrest the cooking, drain and dry them. Dip the mushrooms in the batter, coat well, then deep-fry until golden brown and serve with the following sauce.

Plum Sauce
6tbsp/90ml rice vinegar
4tbsp/60ml sugar
1 small preserved sour plum (Chinese) – available
from oriental stores
1 small red chili, finely chopped
1 small green chili, finely chopped

Gently heat the vinegar and sugar until the sugar dissolves. Break up the preserved plum into the mixture and stir until it thickens. Remove from the heat and allow to cool. Add the chili and pour into a serving dish.

SOUPS

HEALTH

Dotted about the grounds of the Wat Po temple complex near Bangkok's Grand Palace, are a number of sculpture groups which at first sight seem to consist of strangely contorted almost comic figures. These are not meant for entertainment, however. The sculpted figures are there to illustrate the ancient Thai system of massage, for the temple was Thailand's first university where the ancient arts of healing were handed down by the monks. One pavilion at Wat Po is decorated with human figures marked with the pressure points on the body thought to affect certain limbs and organs. Clearly this system is similar to the Chinese discipline of acupuncture. These old skills are still in use today and, in another part of the temple, traditional massage is practised and much appreciated by tired office workers in search of relief from backache or the effects of stress.

The Thai interest in health is both very old and very up-to-the-minute. To the rich legacy of the past the modern Thai citizen has added all the obsessions of the present: health centres, jogging, Nautilus exercise machines and even the city marathon. Not long ago it was decided to inaugurate a new bridge across the

Statues of the Bhudda in one of Bangkok's largest Chinese temples, Wat Mangkhonkamalawat

Chao Phya by making it the starting point for the marathon. The newspaper photographs of the event were startling – literally hundreds of thousands of runners took part, covering the bridge and its approaches in a vast sea of humanity all neatly dressed in T-shirts, shorts and running shoes, all bent on proving that the striving for physical fitness is now as big a preoccupation in Bangkok as it is in London or Los Angeles.

The effect of health awareness on eating habits is becoming more and more apparent. Many young city dwellers in Thailand are starting to take an interest in a controlled diet and while the horrors of industrialized agriculture are not yet a problem in my country, more people are taking to meat-free meals.

Such a regime is far easier to undertake in the East than it is in the West thanks mainly to the presence of the Chinese. There is a large Thai-Chinese community in Bangkok and it often amuses Western visitors to discover that we have our own Chinatown in the Yaowaraj area. Many Thai-Chinese are Buddhists and Chinese Buddhist monks, unlike their Thai counterparts, are strict vegetarians. Out of this grew a great tradition of Chinese vegetarian cooking which is at once practical and poetic: dishes such as the seaweed soup called White Clouds in Blue Sky, or the mushroom dish Silver Bell Buried in Snow.

As well as having this wonderful poetic cookery to hand the Thai vegetarian can rely on the Chinese food markets to provide the raw materials for our own vegetarian dishes. One of the most fascinating markets in Yaowaraj runs along Issaranaphap Lane, a marvellous experience for the vegetarian tourist. Along the narrow lane, already packed with shoppers in the early hours, the food stalls groan with everything you need for a rich and varied vegetarian diet. Most fascinating to me are the beancurd stalls, for tofu lies at the heart of oriental vegetarianism, and in Chinatown it is very special indeed. As the Chinese are never squeamish about food they seem to have decided that a vegetarian should not be totally deprived of meat, and so the beancurd is often shaped into animal forms – a rabbit, a pig, a fish. It is very bizarre and quite contradictory to Western eyes.

If you go to the market you should also visit the Thai Chinese temple Wat Mangkhonkamalawat. This is the largest in Chinatown and you will quickly notice the differences between it and its Thai neighbours. The architecture is typically Chinese as are the statues of gods and other mythological beings and there is something uniquely Chinese in the way the faithful drift round from altar to altar, sanctuary to sanctuary, offering up prayers and incense. Many Chinese make an annual retreat to a temple where they purify the mind with prayer and meditation and the body with a strict vegetarian diet.

The Thai-Chinese are also in the vanguard where healthy exercise is concerned. Early every morning there are sessions of traditional tai chi exercises in the city's one great open space, Lumpini Park. At one time it was only the Chinese community that took part, but today they are joined by groups of Thai joggers and weight lifters, in a great mass of people striving after fitness. As the park is just near my family home I sometimes get up at dawn when I'm staying in Bangkok and take a run round the lawns and flower gardens, passing the parties of elderly Chinese folk stretching and bending to recorded music. For many old people it is the focal point of their lives.

Lumpini Park is very important to my family. My paternal grandfather, a senior civil servant, was given the task of overseeing its creation. King Rama VI, who reigned from 1910 to 1925, had been educated at Oxford University and had ambitious plans for rebuilding Bangkok. He went as far as having a scale model of his ideal city built and my grandfather was given the task of supervising an international exhibition to be held on what was then waste land on the edge of the

Thai medicine – statues in the grounds of Wat Po illustrate the ancient healing art of massage

Tea shop in Bangkok's China town

capital. The King died before the exhibition could take place but his wish that the area should finally become a park was respected. Trees were planted in groups representing their place of origin, there were fretwork pavilions as in European parks and a Chinese-style clock tower was added with the Sino-Thai Solidarity Association paying for a Chinese pavilion.

As time went by the park became the fashionable preserve of Bangkok's high society with ballrooms, amusements and even a floating restaurant. But in recent years it has reverted to what King Rama VI originally intended, a place of recreation for ordinary citizens, and a massive enterprise of restoration and replanting has been undertaken. My grandfather would no doubt be delighted to see how much his labours are appreciated today. In gratitude for what he did he was given a noble title and granted the plot of land near the park where we still live.

One has only to pass a few moments in the crush and noise of modern Bangkok to understand why Lumpini Park is so loved. But better than the joys of exercise is the early morning food market where those who have finished stretching and running can relax and take breakfast. This is a centre for healthy eating where you can enjoy red unpolished rice, vegetable dishes and the usual Thai breakfast of rice soup, hearty and very refreshing after all that strenuous effort. Rice soup is unusual among Thai soups in being a meal in itself, whereas most soups are served as a side dish as part of a full meal. They are meant to be light and refreshing so as to counterbalance heavier, richer dishes. This custom too has its origins in Chinese cuisine where a soup is often served last in a series of dishes, with the intention of refreshing the palate.

The most visible Chinese influence on Thai vegetarian life is the annual Vegetarian Festival on the southern island of Pukhet, held during the Chinese Buddhist Lent when many members of the community forswear meat. There are ceremonies and processions but undoubtedly the oddest of all is one in which young men go into states of trance and when possessed by the gods pierce themselves with sharpened rods, some even sticking a rod through one cheek and out the other. There are other forms of self punishment and some even walk on fire. It is quite alarming to behold and not for the over-sensitive.

VEGETABLE STOCK (BROTH)

These quantities will make a small amount of vegetable stock or broth, enough for one of the soup recipes with a little left over for another dish. However, if you plan to use this book frequently you would do well to consider making a larger amount and either keeping a stockpot going on a regular basis or freezing smaller quantities to use as required.

40fl oz/1.2l/5cups water
1 medium onion (about 4oz/120g), quartered
4oz/120g/2 carrots, roughly chopped
4oz/120g/2 stalks celery, roughly chopped
3–4 coriander roots including the base
or the coriander stem
1tsp/5ml whole black peppercorns

In a large pan boil all the ingredients together and simmer until reduced by about one fifth.

*Early risers practise Tai Chi in Bangkok's Lumpini Park before a
breakfast of rice soup*

RICE SOUP

KHAO TOM

1 garlic clove, coarsely chopped
1tbsp/15ml oil
24fl oz/720ml/3cups vegetable stock (p. 85)
8oz/240g/2cups boiled rice
2oz/60g/^{2}/$_3$cup pre-soaked dried Chinese
mushrooms, finely sliced
1tsp/5ml tang chi, preserved radish
2tbsp/30ml light soy sauce
^{1}/$_2$tsp/2.5ml sugar
1tsp/5ml finely chopped fresh ginger
^{1}/$_2$tsp/2.5ml ground white pepper

To garnish
1 spring onion/scallion, finely chopped
into rings
coriander leaves

In a wok or frying pan heat the oil and fry the garlic until golden brown. Set aside both oil and garlic.

In a large pan, heat the stock, add the boiled rice and bring to the boil. Add all the remaining ingredients down to the pepper, stir well for 30 seconds (slightly longer if you prefer the rice very soft), and turn into a serving bowl. Pour the oil and garlic over the assembled dish, garnish with onion and coriander and serve.

HOT AND SOUR MUSHROOM SOUP

TOM YAM HET

24fl oz/720ml/3cups vegetable stock (p. 85)
1tsp/5ml Nam Prik Pow sauce (p. 140)
1inch/2.5cm lemon grass, finely chopped into rings
3 kaffir lime leaves, roughly torn into three
2tbsp/30ml light soy sauce
1tsp/5ml sugar
2tbsp/30ml lemon juice
2oz/60g/^{2}/$_3$cup oyster mushrooms, coarsely separated
(fresh button mushrooms may be substituted)
2–3 fresh small red or green chilis, slightly
crushed to split open

To garnish
coriander leaves

In a large pan, bring the vegetable stock to the boil and stir in the Nam Prik Pow sauce. Add the remaining ingredients and simmer, stirring well until the mushrooms are just cooked but still al dente. Pour into a serving bowl and garnish with coriander leaves.

BAMBOO SHOOT SOUP

GAENG HONG

1 garlic clove, roughly chopped
2 coriander roots, roughly chopped
1tsp/5ml black peppercorns
1tbsp/15ml oil
24fl oz/720ml/3cups vegetable stock (p. 85)
2oz/60g/^{1}/$_3$cup whole roast peanuts
4oz/120g/^{2}/$_3$cup bamboo shoots, roughly chopped
2tbsp/30ml light soy sauce
1tsp/5ml sugar

In a mortar pound together the garlic, coriander roots and peppercorns to form a paste. In a pan, heat the oil and briefly fry the paste. Pour in the stock, stirring well. Add the peanuts and boil. Simmer for 10 minutes. Add all the remaining ingredients and simmer for a further 5 minutes. Pour into a serving bowl.

SAGO SOUP

GAENG JUD SA KU

24fl oz/720ml/3cups vegetable stock (p. 85)
2tbsp/30ml sago (p. 14)
2oz/60g/^{2}/$_3$cup pre-soaked dried black fungus mushrooms, roughly chopped
2oz/60g/1 small onion, sliced into thin strips
2oz/60g/1 carrot, cut into matchsticks
1tsp/5ml tang chi, preserved radish
2tbsp/30ml light soy sauce
^{1}/$_2$tsp/2.5ml sugar
^{1}/$_2$tsp/2.5ml ground white pepper

To garnish
1 spring onion/scallion, finely chopped into rings
coriander leaves

In a large pan, bring the stock to the boil, add the sago and simmer until the hard sago 'nuts' have become soft and clear. Add all the other ingredients, stirring briefly. Pour into a serving dish and garnish with spring onion and coriander leaves.

BITTER MELON SOUP

GAENG MARA

1 garlic clove, roughly chopped
2 coriander roots, roughly chopped
^{1}/$_2$tsp/2.5ml black peppercorns
1tbsp/15ml oil
24fl oz/720ml/3cups vegetable stock (p. 85)
4oz/120g/1 small bitter melon, cut into 1inch/2.5cm cubes
2oz/60g/^{2}/$_3$cup pre-soaked dried Chinese mushrooms, finely diced
2oz/60g/2 tomatoes, quartered, or cherry tomatoes, halved
2tbsp/30ml light soy sauce
^{1}/$_2$tsp/2.5ml sugar

In a mortar pound the garlic, coriander root and peppercorns to form a paste. In a large pan, heat the oil, briefly fry the paste, add the vegetable stock and bring to the boil, stirring well. Add all the remaining ingredients, stirring constantly until the mushrooms and tomatoes are just cooked.

Sago soup

MIXED VEGETABLE SOUP

JAP CHAI

Where most Thai soups are quickly made once all the ingredients have been prepared, this soup is slowly boiled and meant to be re-heated for consumption over two or three days. The quantities here are sufficient for one day only, so if you would like to use the soup more than once you should multiply the quantities accordingly.

1 garlic clove, roughly chopped
2 coriander roots, roughly chopped
$^1/_2$tsp/2.5ml black peppercorns
2tbsp/30ml oil
2oz/60g/$^2/_3$cup white cabbage, finely shredded
2oz/60g/$^2/_3$cup mooli, white radish, cut into
1inch/2.5cm cubes
2oz/60g/about 2 broccoli stems and florets, coarsely
chopped
2oz/60g/1 stalk celery, coarsely chopped
40fl oz/1.2l/5cups vegetable stock (p. 85)
4oz/120g/1cup ready-fried beancurd, cut into
1inch/2.5cm cubes
2tbsp/30ml light soy sauce
1tbsp/15ml dark soy sauce
1tsp/5ml sugar

In a mortar pound the garlic, coriander roots and peppercorns to form a paste. In a pan, heat the oil and briefly fry the paste. Add the vegetables and briefly stir-fry. Pour the stock over the vegetables and bring to the boil. Add all the remaining ingredients and simmer slowly until all the vegetables are well cooked.

SWEET AND SOUR BEANCURD SOUP

GAENG PREO WAN

24fl oz/720ml/3cups vegetable stock (p. 85)
3tsp/15ml flour
1oz/30g/2 tbsp pickled cabbage (tinned Thai or
Chinese), stems only,
coarsely chopped into 1inch/2.5cm lengths
1oz/30g/$^1/_4$cup bamboo shoots, cut into matchsticks
1oz/30g/about 2 baby sweetcorn, chopped into rings
1oz/30g/1–2tbsp peas
4oz/120g/1cup soft white beancurd, cut into
$^1/_4$inch/6mm cubes
1oz/30g/$^1/_2$ small red or green sweet pepper, finely
chopped
2tbsp/30ml light soy sauce
1tbsp/15ml red vinegar
1tsp/5ml sugar
$^1/_2$tsp/2.5ml ground white pepper

To garnish
coriander leaves

In a large pan, bring the stock to the boil and stir in the flour to slightly thicken. Add the rest of the ingredients in turn, stirring constantly. Turn at once into a serving bowl and garnish with coriander leaves.

BEANCURD (TOFU, TAO HOU)

In common with other oriental cuisines, Thai cookery shuns dairy products. The great substitute is the Chinese invention beancurd or tofu, the water extract of yellow soya beans which is rich in vitamins and minerals. Beancurd is a familiar standby in much Western vegetarian cookery and should already be familiar to most readers. There are three main varieties:

Fresh white beancurd This is bought in blocks weighing about 4oz/120g. It is sold in its own liquid, which is discarded. It is very delicate and will keep in a refrigerator for no more than two days. This is now available in many Western supermarkets and health-food shops.

Ready-fried beancurd Exactly as its name implies, this is white beancurd which has been deep-fried golden brown on the outside. This is available from Chinese stores.

Beancurd sheets These are bought dried in packets and look like wrinkled brown paper. They are very fragile but after soaking for 5–6 minutes you should be able to pull them apart fairly easily. Any torn sections can be patched with other pieces. These are available from Chinese stores.

VERMICELLI SOUP

GAENG WUN SEN

This recipe is a useful way of using up the broken pieces that you inevitably get in a packet of beancurd sheets and would be a sensible follow-up to the recipe for vegetable sausage on p. 72.

1 garlic clove, finely chopped
1tbsp/15ml oil
24fl oz/720ml/3cups vegetable stock (p. 85)
2oz/60g/^{2}/$_3$cup pre-soaked dried black fungus mushrooms, coarsely chopped
2oz/60g/^{1}/$_2$cup beancurd sheet fragments, soaked then drained
4oz/120g vermicelli noodles, coarsely chopped
2 spring onions/scallions, chopped into 1inch/2.5cm lengths
1tsp/5ml tang chi, preserved radish
2tbsp/30ml light soy sauce
^{1}/$_2$tsp/2.5ml sugar
^{1}/$_2$tsp/2.5ml ground white pepper

To garnish
coriander leaves

Make garlic oil: fry the garlic in the oil until golden brown, then set both aside. Bring the stock to the boil, add all the ingredients and simmer briefly. Turn into serving bowls and pour a little garlic oil on to each. Garnish with coriander leaves.

OMELETTE SOUP

GAENG KAIJEOW Ⓔ

1 egg
2tbsp/30ml oil
24fl oz/720ml/3cups vegetable stock (p. 85)
2oz/60g/1 carrot, chopped into small cubes
1tsp/5ml tang chi, preserved radish
2 spring onions/scallions, chopped into 1inch/2.5cm lengths
2tbsp/30ml light soy sauce
^{1}/$_2$tsp/2.5ml sugar
^{1}/$_2$tsp/2.5ml ground white pepper

To garnish
coriander leaves

Beat the egg, heat the oil in a small omelette pan and make a firm omelette. Remove the omelette from the pan, roll into a cylinder and cut into $\frac{1}{4}$inch/6mm thick rounds. Secure the rounds with a tiny skewer or tooth-pick and set aside.

Put the stock and the carrots into a large pan and bring to the boil. Simmer for 5 minutes, then add all the remaining ingredients ending with the omelette rounds. Stir, then pour into a serving bowl and garnish with coriander leaves.

Vermicelli soup

PICKLED VEGETABLE SOUP

GAENG GONG CHAI

24fl oz/720ml/3cups vegetable stock (p. 85)
2oz/60g/²/₃cup pre-soaked dried
Chinese mushrooms, finely sliced
4oz/120g/1 cup pickled cabbage (tinned Thai or
Chinese), stems only,
chopped into 1inch/2.5cm lengths
2tbsp/30ml light soy sauce
2tsp/10ml sugar
¹/₂tsp/2.5ml ground white pepper

In a large pan, bring the vegetable stock to the boil, add all the ingredients and cook, stirring constantly, until the mushrooms are just al dente. Pour into a serving bowl.

FRIED WHITE CABBAGE SOUP

GAENG GARAM BEE TOD

2tbsp/30ml oil
2 white cabbage wedges (4oz/120g each)
24fl oz/720ml/3cups vegetable stock (p. 85)
1tsp/5ml tang chi, preserved radish
2tbsp/30ml light soy sauce
¹/₂tsp/2.5ml sugar
¹/₂tsp/2.5ml ground white pepper

In a wok or frying pan/skillet, heat the oil and fry the two cabbage wedges until they are beginning to brown. Remove and put into a large pan filled with the vegetable stock, bring to the boil and add the remaining ingredients. Simmer until the cabbage is al dente.

POTATO AND SHALLOT SOUP

TOM JILL

24fl oz/720ml/3cups vegetable stock (p. 85)
8oz/230g/2–3 peeled potatoes, cut into 1inch/2.5cm
cubes
3 small shallots, finely chopped into rings
2 dried Chinese mushrooms, soaked, drained and
finely chopped
1oz/30g/1 large carrot, cut lengthways into 'planks',
then across into 1inch/2.5cm squares, or stamped
into shapes with a vegetable cutter
¹/₄tsp/1.5ml chili powder
¹/₂tsp/2.5ml sugar
2tbsp/30ml light soy sauce
2tbsp/30ml lemon juice
2 small red or green chilis, slightly crushed
10 sweet basil leaves

Put the stock and the potatoes into a large pan, bring to the boil and simmer until almost cooked. Add the remaining ingredients in turn, stirring briefly between each addition. Turn into a serving bowl.

CUCUMBER AND EGG SOUP

GAENG JUD TANG GWA Ⓔ

When I first came to the West as a student my new friends would ask me to cook something Thai. At the time this was no easy task as even basic ingredients were hard to come by. I soon discovered that this was the easiest dish to make with the sort of materials usually available in Western kitchens. If you cannot find the tang chi, do as I used to and add an extra tablespoon of soy sauce.

24fl oz/720ml/3cups vegetable stock (p. 85)
6oz/180g/about ¹/₂cucumber, quartered lengthways
then chopped
into 1inch/2.5cm wedges
1 egg
2 spring onions/scallions, chopped into 1inch/2.5cm
lengths
2tbsp/30ml light soy sauce
¹/₂tsp/2.5ml sugar
1tsp/5ml tang chi, preserved radish
¹/₂tsp/2.5ml ground white pepper

To garnish
coriander leaves

Bring the stock to the boil and add the cucumber wedges. Break the egg into the liquid, stirring slowly so that it poaches in broken strands. Add all the other ingredients and return to the boil. Simmer for 1 minute. Turn into a serving bowl and garnish with coriander.

YOUNG TAMARIND LEAF SOUP

TOM YAM BAI MAKAM

If the previous dish is the easiest to make, then this is surely the most difficult. Young tamarind leaf is virtually impossible to find outside Asia – however, you *can* substitute watercress for the tamarind leaves to make something admittedly different but still very delicious.

24fl oz/720ml/3cups vegetable stock (p. 85)
1inch/2.5cm lemon grass, finely chopped into rings
3 kaffir lime leaves, roughly torn up
4 small fresh red or green chilis, roughly crushed
¹/₂tsp/2.5ml sugar
2tbsp/30ml lemon juice
2tbsp/30ml light soy sauce
4oz/120g/1 bunch young tamarind leaves (or
watercress)

Bring the stock to the boil, add the lemon grass and lime leaves and simmer briefly. Add the chilis, sugar, lemon juice and soy sauce and simmer briefly. At the last moment add the tamarind leaves or watercress, stir once, turn into a serving bowl and bring immediately to the table.

*Ordeal by fire – in a trance-like state devotees at Phuket's
vegetarian festival demonstrate mind-over-matter*

CAULIFLOWER, COCONUT AND GALANGAL SOUP

TOM KA

4fl oz/120ml/$^1/_2$cup coconut milk
1inch/2.5cm lemon grass, finely chopped into rings
1inch/2.5cm galangal, finely chopped into rings
3 kaffir lime leaves, roughly torn into quarters
8oz/230g/1 small cauliflower, cut into florets
2tbsp/15ml light soy sauce
1tsp/5ml sugar
24fl oz/720ml/3cups vegetable stock (p. 85)
4 fresh small red or green chilis, slightly crushed
2tbsp/30ml lemon juice

To garnish
coriander leaves

In a large pan heat the coconut milk with the lemon grass, galangal, kaffir lime leaves, cauliflower, soy sauce, sugar and stock, and simmer until the cauliflower florets are al dente. Remove from the heat and add the chilis and lemon juice. Stir once, pour into a serving bowl and garnish with coriander leaves.

WHITE BEANCURD SOUP

GAENG JUD TAO HOU KOW

24fl oz/720ml/3cups vegetable stock (p. 85)
1tsp/5ml tang chi, preserved radish
4oz/120g/1 cup soft white beancurd, cut into
$^1/_2$inch/1.25cm cubes
2tbsp/30ml light soy sauce
$^1/_2$tsp/2.5ml sugar
$^1/_2$tsp/2.5ml ground white pepper
2 spring onions/scallions, chopped into 1inch/2.5cm
lengths

To garnish
coriander leaves

In a large pan bring the vegetable stock to the boil, add the tang chi and simmer briefly. Add all the remaining ingredients, stir briefly and serve garnished with coriander.

CURRIES

THE SPICE TRADE

A short walk from my family home, in the Saladaeng area of Bangkok, is one of the city's most revered Hindu Temples. In the dark cave-like sanctuary Brahmin priests tend the sacred fire, which they bring out for the waiting supplicants who come with gifts of fruit and flowers. Most of those waiting for the blessing of fire are Thais. The Indian population of Thailand is quite small, though the influence of India itself is much larger. When the Thai people had settled in their new land, after their migration from China, waves of missionaries arrived from India bringing Buddhism and Hinduism. While Buddhism became our formal faith, traces of the gods and legends of Hinduism still remain, such as the honour done to the Rice Mother, Mae Posop, mentioned in the first chapter.

Many of our royal ceremonies are Brahmin in origin, in particular the annual rice ceremony attended by the King, in which a bullock is offered a series of gifts, the one chosen being a sign of the quality of the coming year's harvest. At a more personal level, every house, indeed every building in Thailand, has a small 'spirit house' offered as a dwelling place for the spirit of the land, who has been displaced and must be placated.

The greatest influence of India on our cuisine has been in the use of the spices brought by the original

A massaman curry in the sumptuous setting of the Wat Raja Bopitr, a temple built in the nineteenth century in a blend of Thai and Western forms.

missionaries. As a people who already liked spicy food it was a certainty that we would be attracted to these new flavours. However, when you eat a Thai curry you will be struck immediately by the fact that it bears little resemblance to the thick, rich Indian curries with which you are familiar. The explanation is simple – the spices used by the Indians who came to Thailand as missionaries were not those used today. The chili was introduced to the East only in the sixteenth century when the Portuguese brought it from South America. Before that 'heat' was obtained through pepper and mustard seed. The thick curries of India are a fairly new phenomenon; what we in Thailand inherited, and still have today, are what are quaintly called the pre-medieval curries, which are thin and soup-like. The advantage of these curries is that they are light and quick to cook as they require no stewing.

Curries in Thailand are always part of a selection of dishes in a main meal and never served on their own. Their heat is usually counterbalanced by a blander flavoured or sweeter dish. I have put them into a separate chapter for convenience, as you will have to go to some trouble to acquire and prepare the spices needed for the various curry pastes, and if you do decide to undertake this task you will probably be so pleased with the results that you will want to make more than one curry. With the 'medieval curry' you are in the heart of true Asian cuisine with all the romantic echoes of the spice trade and the voyages that brought those wonderful tastes and aromas to the West.

One of the most appealing places to eat in Bangkok is the Spice Market Restaurant in the Regent Hotel with its bottles and jars bearing the romantic names that recall the great trade – star anise, krachai, galangal. A walk in the older parts of Bangkok near the river casts up sights to stir the heart – a glimpse into a darkened shop-house, all old polished wood like a ship's hull, in which you can just see the sacks of cumin, cinnamon and cardamom, and where you can smell the real aromatic treasures of the East.

CHICKPEA CURRY
GAENG KARI TUA

This is an unusual dish as beans are not very common in Thai cookery. I found this particular curry on a visit to a country temple – Wat Pratom Asoke, the centre of a forest monastery near the country town of Nakhon Pathom, west of Bangkok. The order of monks at the temple is vegetarian and they work on the land growing their own food. With such hard work they need to ensure a high protein level in their diet, hence this useful and tasty recipe. Because of the varied work at Wat Pratom Asoke some of the lay workers come to eat in the open-air kitchen at odd hours, and a large bowl of chickpea curry is left waiting for anyone who needs it. It is a dish that can be prepared in advance and re-heated.

1 garlic clove, coarsely chopped
2 coriander roots, coarsely chopped
$^1/_2$tsp/2.5ml whole black peppercorns
2tbsp/30ml oil
8fl oz/240ml/1cup coconut milk
1tbsp/15ml curry powder
4oz/120g/1 potato, peeled and cut into 1inch/2.5cm cubes
8fl oz/240ml/1cup chickpeas, soaked overnight or straight from a tin
4oz/120g/2 tomatoes sliced into wedges
10 sweet basil leaves
2tbsp/30ml light soy sauce
$^1/_2$tsp/2.5ml salt
1tsp/5ml sugar

In a mortar, pound the garlic, coriander roots and peppercorns to form a paste. Heat the oil and briefly fry the paste, then add the coconut milk, stirring well. Stir in the remaining ingredients in order, bring to the boil and simmer until the potatoes and chickpeas are cooked al dente.

A dish of chickpea curry in the traditional kitchen of Wat Pratom Asoke near Nakhon Pathom

POTATO CURRY

GAENG KARI

As rice eaters we have never really taken to the potato – our word for it, 'man', means sweet potato and to indicate the American variety we say 'man farang', which literally means foreign potato. The main use we find for the foreign potato is as potato crisps/chips, but this recipe is a rare exception where the vegetable is allowed to stand on its own.

1tsp/5ml coriander seeds
2tsp/10ml finely chopped galangal
2tsp/10ml finely chopped lemon grass
2tsp/10ml finely chopped garlic
2tbsp/30ml oil
8fl oz/240ml/1 cup coconut milk
8oz/230g/about 2 potatoes, peeled and cut into 1inch/2.5cm cubes
2tbsp/30ml light soy sauce
1tsp/5ml sugar
$1/2$tsp/2.5ml salt
1tbsp/15ml curry powder
4fl oz/120ml/$1/2$cup vegetable stock (p. 85)
6oz/230g/about 4 small onions, halved

In a mortar, pound the coriander seeds, galangal, lemon grass and garlic together to form a paste. Heat the oil, stir in the paste and immediately add the coconut milk. Stir briefly, then add the potatoes and the soy sauce, sugar, salt, and curry powder; stir well. Boil, add the vegetable stock, return to the boil, add the onion halves and simmer until the potatoes are cooked al dente.

MORNING GLORY CURRY

GAENG TE PO

2tbsp/30ml oil
1garlic clove, finely chopped
1tbsp/5ml red curry paste (p. 105)
8fl oz/240ml/1 cup coconut milk
4oz/120g/1 $1/3$cups oyster mushrooms, chopped
4oz/120g/1 cup ready-fried beancurd sliced into 2×$1/2$inch/5×1.25cm strips
3 kaffir lime leaves, coarsely chopped
1 small kaffir lime, halved
$1/2$tsp/2.5ml salt
1tbsp/15ml tamarind juice (or 2tbsp/30ml lemon juice)
1tbsp/15ml light soy sauce
1tsp/5ml sugar
4fl oz/120ml/$1/2$cup vegetable stock (p. 85)
4oz/120g/1 bunch morning glory, coarsely chopped into 1inch/2.5cm lengths

In a frying pan/skillet or wok, heat the oil and fry the garlic until golden brown. Stir in the curry paste and immediately add the coconut milk, stirring well. Add the other ingredients in turn, up to and including the sugar, stirring constantly. Boil, add the vegetable stock and boil again. Add the morning glory and simmer until cooked al dente.

RED CURRY PASTE
NAM PRIK GAENG DAENG

This is the most commonly used paste in Thai cookery, not merely for curries but for many other dishes in this book. If you intend to use this book frequently it would be prudent to increase the quantities given here in order to make a stock to use as and when you need it. The paste will keep for up to three weeks in a sealed container in a refrigerator.

7 large dried red chilis
2tsp/10ml coriander seeds
2tsp/10ml finely chopped galangal root
2tsp/10ml finely chopped lemon grass
1tsp/5ml salt
1tbsp/15ml finely chopped kaffir lime peel
2tbsp/30ml finely chopped garlic
2tbsp/30ml finely chopped shallots

In a large mortar, pound all the ingredients together in turn to form a thick paste.

NORTHERN CURRY

GAENG HO

The word 'ho' implies that everything has been 'thrown in', and this dish from the northern capital of Chiang Mai provides a way of using up any left over food from the day before.

2tbsp/30ml oil
1tbsp/15ml red curry paste (p. 105)
1tsp/5ml finely chopped lemon grass
1tsp/5ml finely chopped galangal
2 shallots, finely chopped
2oz/60g/ $^1/_3$ cup bamboo shoots, cut into matchsticks
4oz/120g vermicelli noodles, soaked, drained and coarsely chopped
2oz/60g/1 small bundle long beans, roughly chopped into 1inch/2.5cm lengths
2oz/60g/about $^1/_2$ purple aubergine/eggplant, roughly chopped,
or 10 pea aubergines (p. 56)
3 kaffir lime leaves
3tbsp/45ml light soy sauce
1tsp/5ml sugar
2 large fresh red chilis, finely sliced on the diagonal
20 red basil leaves

Heat the oil, briefly fry the paste then quickly add all the ingredients in turn, stirring between each addition. There should be sufficient water from the soaked noodles to permit cooking, if not add a little vegetable stock (3tbsp/45ml should be sufficient). As soon as the red basil leaves have been stirred in, pour into a serving bowl.

MIXED VEGETABLE CURRY

GAENG PED PAK

2tbsp/30ml oil
1tbsp/15ml red curry paste (p. 105)
8fl oz/240ml/1cup coconut milk
2oz/60g/ $^1/_3$ cup bamboo shoots, roughly chopped
2oz/60g/about 2 whole baby sweetcorn
2oz/60g/1 small bundle long beans, chopped into 1inch/2.5cm lengths
2oz/60g/about $^1/_2$ purple aubergine/eggplant, chopped into 1inch/2.5cm rounds, then halved
2oz/60g/about $^1/_4$ cauliflower, cut into florets
1tbsp/15ml light soy sauce
1tsp/5ml salt
1tsp/5ml sugar
3 kaffir lime leaves
2 large fresh red chilis, cut lengthways into thin slivers
15 red basil leaves

Heat the oil, briefly fry the paste, add the coconut milk and stir well. Add the other ingredients, stirring well, until the vegetables are cooked al dente.

Mixed vegetable curry, with grilled curried rice in the Regent Hotel's Spice Market Restaurant

CHIANG MAI CURRY

GAENG HAENG LAY

This is a recipe from my London restaurant, The Chiang Mai, which specializes in northern Thai cuisine.

2tbsp/30ml oil
1tbsp/15ml red curry paste (p. 105)
4oz/120g/1cup ready-fried beancurd, roughly chopped
into 1inch/2.5cm strips
$^{1}/_{2}$tsp/2.5ml turmeric powder
4tbsp/60ml coconut milk
3oz/90g/1 cup pre-soaked dried
Chinese mushroom coarsely chopped
1tbsp/15ml lemon juice
1tbsp/15ml light soy sauce
1tsp/5ml sugar
$^{1}/_{2}$tsp/2.5ml salt
1inch/2.5cm piece ginger root, peeled and cut into matchsticks
1 whole head pickled garlic, finely sliced across the
bulb to make flower-shaped sections
2oz/60g/1 tomato, cut into segments

To garnish
coriander leaves

Heat the oil and briefly stir in the paste. Add all the other ingredients in turn, stirring briefly between each addition. Immediately turn into a serving bowl and garnish with coriander.

JUNGLE CURRY

GAENG PA

2tbsp/10ml oil
1tbsp/5ml red curry paste (p. 105)
1oz/30g/1 small piece krachai, lesser ginger, cut
into matchsticks
(if dried soak for 30 minutes before use)
8fl oz/240ml/1cup vegetable stock (p. 85)
2oz/60g/1 small bundle long beans, chopped into
1inch/2.5cm lengths
2oz/60g/1 carrot, cut into matchsticks
2oz/60g/about 2 baby sweetcorn (halved if large)
2 kaffir lime leaves
2 small fresh red or green chilis, thinly sliced on the
diagonal
2tbsp/30ml light soy sauce
1tsp/5ml sugar
$^{1}/_{2}$tsp/2.5ml salt
2oz/60g/about $^{1}/_{2}$ purple aubergine/eggplant, sliced
into rounds 1inch/2.5cm thick,
then halved

Heat the oil and briefly fry the curry paste, add the krachai and vegetable stock and stir briefly. Add all the remaining ingredients down to and including the salt, stirring constantly. Add the aubergines last and simmer briefly until they are cooked al dente.

DRY CURRY MUSHROOMS

PENAENG HET

The dry curry paste
10 dried long red chilis, deseeded and finely
chopped
5 small shallots, chopped
2tbsp/30ml coarsely chopped garlic
2 stalks lemon grass, coarsely chopped
1inch/2.5cm galangal, coarsely chopped
1tsp/5ml ground coriander seeds
1tsp/5ml ground cumin
3 coriander roots, coarsely chopped
2tbsp/30ml roast peanuts

In a large mortar, pound all the ingredients together until you have a smooth paste.

The curry
2tbsp/30ml oil
1 garlic clove, finely chopped
2tsp/10ml dry curry paste (above)
4fl oz/120ml/¹⁄₂ cup coconut milk
8oz/240g/2²⁄₃ cups pre-soaked dried
Chinese mushrooms, drained and coarsely chopped
2oz/60g/1 small bundle long beans, chopped into
1inch/2.5cm lengths
2 kaffir lime leaves, rolled into cigarettes and
extra-finely sliced
2tbsp/30ml light soy sauce
1tsp/5ml sugar
1tbsp/15ml coarsely ground roast peanuts
15 red basil leaves

Heat the oil and fry the garlic until golden brown. Add the curry paste and stir briefly. Add the coconut milk and stir well, then add the remaining ingredients in order, stirring constantly. As soon as the basil leaves have been stirred in, turn into a bowl, and serve.

BITTER MELON CURRY

GAENG OM

2tbsp/30ml oil
1tbsp/15ml red curry paste (p. 105)
8fl oz/240ml/1 cup coconut milk
1tbsp/5ml finely chopped lemon grass
1tsp/5ml finely chopped galangal
2 small shallots, finely chopped
1 large dried red chili, finely chopped into rings
2oz/60g/¹⁄₂ cup pieces of broken beancurd sheet
(weight after soaking)
4oz/120g/1¹⁄₃ cups button mushrooms, halved
6oz/180g/about ¹⁄₂ bitter melon, chopped into
1inch/2.5cm
segments and the seeds scooped out
2tbsp/30ml light soy sauce
1tsp/10ml sugar
¹⁄₂ tsp/5ml salt

Heat the oil and briefly fry the red curry paste. Add the coconut milk and stir. Add the remaining ingredients, stirring constantly. Simmer until the bitter melon is cooked al dente.

SOUR VEGETABLE CURRY

GAENG SOM

The paste
3 large dried red chilis, finely chopped
2tsp/10ml finely chopped krachai, lesser ginger
2tsp/10ml finely chopped garlic
2tsp/10ml finely chopped shallots

Pound all the ingredients together in a mortar to form a paste.

The curry
4oz/120g/1 $^1/_3$ cups button mushrooms
2tbsp/30ml oil
8fl oz/240ml/1cup vegetable stock (p. 85)
2oz/60g/1 small piece mooli, white radish, finely sliced (and halved if very large)
2oz/60g/about $^1/_3$ green papaya, finely sliced to make thin 'planks', then cut into 1inch/2.5cm squares
2oz/60g/1 small bundle long beans, cut into 1inch/2.5cm lengths
2oz/60g/about 5 Chinese cabbage leaves, coarsely chopped into 1inch/2.5cm strands
1tsp/5ml tamarind juice (or 2tsp/10ml lemon juice)
2tbsp/30ml light soy sauce
1tsp/5ml sugar
$^1/_2$tsp/2.5ml salt

In a mortar pound the mushrooms until well mashed and set aside. Heat the oil and briefly fry the curry paste, add the stock and boil, stirring well. Add the mashed mushrooms and stir well to blend. Add the remaining ingredients and simmer until the vegetables are cooked al dente.

Sour vegetable curry

Pineapple curry with fried curried rice

PINEAPPLE CURRY

GAENG KUA SAPPAROT

The halved pineapple shells may be used as bowls in which to serve the curry.

The paste
5 large dried red chilis, finely chopped
2tbsp/30ml finely chopped garlic
1tbsp/15ml finely chopped galangal
2tbsp/30ml finely chopped lemon grass
1tsp/5ml finely chopped coriander root
1tsp/5ml finely chopped kaffir lime peel
1tsp/5ml finely chopped krachai, lesser ginger
2tbsp/30ml finely chopped shallots
1tsp/5ml salt

Pound the ingredients together in a mortar to form a paste.

The curry
2tbsp/30ml oil
1 garlic clove, finely chopped
1tbsp/15ml curry paste (above)
8fl oz/240ml/1cup coconut milk
10oz/300g/about 1 fresh pineapple, cut into segments
2 kaffir lime leaves, halved
1tsp/5ml finely chopped kaffir lime peel
2tbsp/30ml lemon juice
2tsp/10ml sugar, or to taste
1tbsp/15ml light soy sauce
$^{1}/_{2}$tsp/2.5ml salt

Heat the oil and fry the garlic until golden brown. Briefly fry the curry paste and immediately add the coconut milk, stirring well. Slowly bring to the boil, then add the other ingredients, stirring constantly. Turn into a bowl or the scooped out shells of the pineapple and serve.

112

GREEN CURRY WITH AUBERGINE AND COCONUT

GAENG KEOW WAN

If you cannot get fresh young coconut, it is available tinned. Bamboo shoots can also be used in its place.

The green curry paste
1tbsp/15ml finely chopped lemon grass
1tbsp/15ml black peppercorns
1tbsp/15ml finely chopped coriander root
10 small green chilis
1tsp/5ml ground cumin
1tsp/5ml coarsely chopped galangal
1tsp/5ml coriander seeds
2tbsp/30ml coarsely chopped shallots
2tbsp/30ml coarsely chopped garlic
1tsp/5ml chopped fresh kaffir lime peel

In a mortar pound all the ingredients together until a soft paste forms.

The green curry
2tbsp/30ml oil
1tbsp/15ml green curry paste (above)
8fl oz/240ml/1 cup coconut milk
4fl oz/120ml/$^1/_2$ cup vegetable stock (p. 85)
3oz/90g/$^2/_3$cups quartered round or pea aubergine/
eggplant (p. 56)
3oz/90g/1 cup straw mushrooms, halved if large
4oz/120g/about $^1/_2$ young soft coconut, flesh only, cut
into 1inch/2.5cm blocks
1tsp/5ml salt
1tbsp/15ml sugar
3 kaffir lime leaves, coarsely chopped
3 small fresh red or green chilis, chopped
on the diagonal
15 red basil leaves

Heat the oil, add the curry paste, briefly stir then add the coconut milk and stir well. Add the remaining ingredients in turn, stirring constantly. As soon as the red basil leaves have been stirred in, serve.

SULTAN'S CURRY

GAENG LUANG

This recipe has no coconut milk to balance the chilis, so you may wish to reduce the amount of chilis in the paste.

The paste
2oz/60g/about 1 head garlic, coarsely chopped
2oz/60g/about 1 root fresh turmeric
4oz/120g/about 6 shallots
1tsp/5ml black peppercorns
2oz/60g/about 4 fresh yellow or red chilis

In a mortar, pound together all the ingredients to form a paste.

The curry
1tbsp/15ml uncooked rice grains
8fl oz/240ml/1cup vegetable stock (p. 85)
1tbsp/5ml curry paste (above)
4oz/120g/$^2/_3$cup pickled bamboo shoots, sliced
3oz/90g/1 small bundle long beans, chopped into
1inch/2.5cm lengths
3oz/90g//1 cup straw mushrooms, halved if large
2tbsp/30ml light soy sauce
2tbsp/30ml lemon juice
1tsp/5ml sugar
$^1/_2$tsp/2.5ml salt

In a mortar, pound the uncooked rice grains to a fine powder and set aside.

In a pan, heat the vegetable stock, add the curry paste and stir well. Bring to the boil, add the powdered rice, stir, then add all the remaining ingredients, stirring constantly. Cook until the vegetables are al dente.

MASSAMAN CURRY

MASSAMAN

Massaman or muslim curry is, as its name implies, from the South of Thailand where we share a border with our Islamic neighbours in Malaysia. Influences of their cooking, the rich dark flavours, the use of nut sauces, have inevitably crossed into our cuisine – especially in satay. This is about the nearest curry in the Thai repertoire to the sort of Indian curries most people are now familiar with.

The Massaman paste
10 dried long red chilis, deseeded and chopped
1tsp/5ml ground coriander seeds
1tsp/5ml ground cumin
1tsp/5ml ground cinnamon
1tsp/5ml ground cloves
1tsp/5ml ground star anise
1tsp/5ml ground cardamom
1tsp/5ml ground white pepper
4tbsp/60ml/6 small shallots, roughly chopped
4tbsp/60ml/7 small garlic cloves, roughly chopped
2inch/5cm piece lemon grass, chopped
$^1/_2$inch/1.25cm piece galangal, chopped
1tbsp/15ml chopped kaffir lime peel
1tsp/15ml salt

In a large mortar pound together the ingredients a few at a time, working them well in to form a soft paste.

The curry
2tbsp/30ml oil
1 small garlic clove, finely chopped
1tbsp/30ml curry paste (above)
8fl oz/240ml/1cup coconut milk
4oz/120g/$^2/_3$cup whole roast peanuts
4oz/120g/1–2 potatoes, peeled and chopped into
1inch/2.5cm cubes
6oz/180g/1$^1/_3$cups ready-fried beancurd, chopped
into 1inch/2.5cm cubes
3 whole small shallots
1tbsp/30ml tamarind juice, or
2tbsp/60ml lemon juice
1tsp/5ml salt
1tbsp/30ml sugar

Heat the oil and fry the garlic until golden brown. Add the curry paste, stir briefly then add the coconut milk and stir well. Add all the remaining ingredients in turn and simmer for 15 to 20 minutes until the potatoes are cooked al dente.

By the Chao Phya River, the headquarters of the East Asiatic Company founded by a Danish sailor at the turn of the century

MAIN DISHES

THE PALACE ON THE HILL

The kings of Thailand have been great builders of monuments. From the elegant spires of the Grand Palace in Bangkok to the colossal Chedi in Nakhon Pathom, said to be the tallest Buddhist monument in the world, the entire country is graced with richly decorated temples and imposing royal residences. Each succeeding monarch has enjoyed creating a new retreat of his own, for some a summer palace, for others a country lodge or seaside villa. But none is as beautiful or as dramatically situated as the stunning white palace built in 1858 by King Mongkut (Rama IV) on the summit of a hill outside the town of Petchaburi.

When I first saw the palace it had long been abandoned and parts of it were crumbling away. Happily the past six years have seen a mammoth labour of reconstruction by the national Fine Arts Department, which has returned the buildings to their former glory. Even the original furnishings and art objects have been restored, so that it is now possible to see this unusual royal home as its creator intended. Indeed, the palace is far more than just a building, it is a physical manifestation of the philosophy of the extraordinary man who

The temple of Phra Nakhon Khiri, the Great Palace, built by King Mongkut on a hill planted with frangipani

117

built it. King Mongkut was the first of the great modernizing kings of Thailand, and his work was carried on by his son King Chulalongkorn (Rama V).

Although he was the model for the monarch in *The King and I*, in reality King Mongkut was a highly intelligent man, largely self-taught, who attempted almost single-handedly to set his deeply traditional country on the path of progress. Unlike his son, Mongkut never

Transforming a rose apple into a leaf and a potato into a delicate flower in easy stages – you will need a very sharp, pointed knife

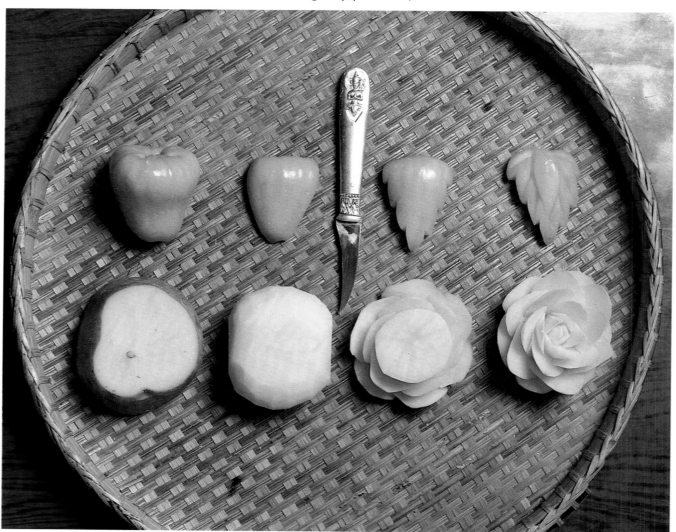

had an opportunity to visit Europe to see for himself the many advances in science and manufacturing he so eagerly read about. But he had an idea of how nineteenth-century Western society must have been and was determined to recreate what he could imagine of it in Siam. The hill he found was named Maha Sawan or Great Heaven, and the palace he planned for its summit was conceived as an intriguing mix of European and Asian elements.

The King's architect was much influenced by the British and Chinese colonial buildings in Singapore, then Siam's nearest point of contact with Western ideas, but somehow the palace managed to achieve an intriguingly Mediterranean look; at first sight it could almost be Spanish or Portuguese. Look one way and there is a seaside villa of vivid white walls and columns with tiered terrace gardens and tree-shaded walks, but turn round and you find yourself facing the thin spires and bell-shaped stupa of a traditional Thai temple. Yet somehow these strange encounters make a harmonious whole, which was precisely the King's intention. Siam, so the building seems to say, could be modern and yet have its own culture.

This ability to marry East with West is to me typically Thai. It is one of our abiding strengths, and one which has helped us survive as an independent nation when the lands around us were overrun. In the palace, you can see this marriage most poignantly in the royal dining room, which offers stunning views over the valley with its pattern of rice fields stretching to the distant mountains that mark our western border with Burma. Nothing could be more oriental, yet it was in that room that the King and his guests dined off the finest European porcelain and sipped their French champagne and German wines from Baccarat crystal that had made the long sea voyage from Marseilles.

At that time Thai haute cuisine was very much the preserve of royal and noble families and the divide between the elaborate, highly decorated dishes set before the monarch and the basic food eaten by a peasant farmer was enormous. Today, thanks to that modernization of the country which came as a result of King Mongkut's endeavours, there is a large Thai middle class. One result of this has been the spread and adaptation of that once select cookery into a cuisine for all. When you eat in a Thai restaurant you are enjoying a fairly recent phenomenon. And this democratization of Thai cuisine even extends to what was once the most rarified of culinary arts, the intricate carving of fruit and vegetables into delicate flowers to decorate a dish. Once found only in the royal kitchens, today's skilled carvers are likely to be working for one of the big hotels where their creations decorate buffets and special presentations.

Thai cookery is far from a rigid affair, no two Thai cooks produce exactly the same dish and I hope you will feel free to adapt and experiment with the recipes here. Questioning and experiment were exactly what King Mongkut wanted to encourage. One of the more fascinating buildings at the hilltop palace is a round tower from which the King could pursue his study of astronomy. Indeed, in 1868, he successfully predicted an eclipse of the sun and helped put an end to the ancient superstition that the sun had been swallowed by a dragon who would only regurgitate it if disturbed by the loud beating of drums and gongs. Since their restoration, the palace and its surrounding gardens have been renamed the Phra Nakhon Khiri Historical Park and to help visitors get to the summit two cable cars have been installed; how the ever inquisitive King Mongkut would have been fascinated by them. One of the things that most intrigued him when he listened to the reports of the ambassadors he sent to Europe was the wondrous tale of snow in winter. Intent on seeing for himself what such a thing might be like, he had the entire hillside around the palace planted with white frangipani which blossom and scatter their petals in December. Thus, during the European winter King Mongkut could look out on his mountain covered in a layer of snow.

SPICY QUICK-FRIED LONG BEANS

PAT PRIK KING

3oz/90g/1³/₄cups ready-fried beancurd
finely sliced
oil for deep-frying
2tbsp/30ml oil
1tsp/5ml finely chopped garlic
1tbsp/15ml red curry paste (p. 105)
8oz/230g/1 bundle long beans, chopped into
1inch/2.5cm lengths
2tbsp/30ml light soy sauce
4tbsp/60ml vegetable stock (p. 85)
1tsp/5ml sugar
1tbsp/15ml ground roast peanuts
2 kaffir lime leaves, finely chopped

Deep-fry the beancurd until the white sides are golden brown, drain and set aside. In a wok or frying pan/skillet heat the 2tbsp/30ml oil, fry the garlic until golden brown, then stir in the red curry paste. Add all the remaining ingredients, ending with the beancurd. Stir briefly and serve.

CHILI PUMPKIN

PAT PET FAK TONG

Pumpkin can usually be bought in wedges. Cut off the hard outer layer, scoop out the seeds and use the softer flesh inside.

2tbsp/30ml oil
1tsp/5ml finely chopped garlic
4 small fresh red or green chilis, finely chopped
3 kaffir lime leaves, roughly chopped
10oz/300g/about ¹/₂ medium pumpkin, cut into

1 × ¹/₄inch/25×6mm cubes
2tbsp/30ml light soy sauce
1tsp/5ml sugar
4tbsp/60ml vegetable stock (p. 85)
20 whole red basil leaves

In a wok or frying pan/skillet, heat the oil, and fry the garlic and chilis until the garlic is golden brown. Add all the remaining ingredients in turn, stirring constantly. Turn on to a serving dish.

PALM HEARTS WITH KAFFIR LIME LEAF

YOD MAPROW PAD KIMOW

2tbsp/30ml oil
1tsp/5ml finely chopped garlic
4 small fresh red or green chilis,
finely chopped
6oz/180g/1 ¹/₂cups hearts of palm, chopped into
rings
¹/₂inch/1.25cm thick
4oz/120g/1 ¹/₃cups straw mushrooms
1tbsp/15ml light soy sauce
1tsp/5ml dark soy sauce
1tsp/5ml sugar
1oz/30g/2tbsp whole green peppercorns
2oz/60g/¹/₄ cup sweet peppers, finely sliced
into thin strips
3tbsp/45ml vegetable stock (p. 85)
3 kaffir lime leaves, coarsely chopped
15 whole red basil leaves

Heat the oil, fry the garlic until golden brown and add the remaining ingredients in turn, stirring constantly until the vegetables are cooked al dente. Turn on to a serving dish.

Palm hearts with kaffir lime leaf

YELLOW BEAN SPICY DIP WITH CRUDITES

TOW JEOW LON

The crudités
*Any crisp fresh vegetables will do:
cucumber, Chinese cabbage, long beans, etc.*

Chop the crudités into small convenient portions, arrange on a serving platter and set aside.

The dip
*4oz/120g/$^2/_3$ cup yellow bean sauce, drained to
remove excess liquid
8fl oz/240ml/1 cup coconut milk
2 small shallots, finely chopped
4oz/120g/1$^1/_3$ cups button mushrooms, finely
chopped
1tbsp/15ml tamarind juice, or 2tbsp/30ml lemon
juice
2tsp/10ml sugar
1tbsp/15ml light soy sauce
2 large fresh red chilis, sliced lengthways
into fine matchsticks*

In a mortar, briefly pound the drained yellow beans until broken up, and set aside. In a pan, heat the coconut milk then add the mashed yellow beans, stir well, and add all the remaining ingredients down to and including the soy sauce. Bring to the boil and simmer briefly. Remove from the heat, stir in the chili matchsticks. Turn into a bowl and serve with the crudités.

FRIED BEANCURD WITH GARLIC AND PEPPER

TAO HOU GRATIAM PRIK THAI

*2tsp/10ml coarsely chopped garlic
1tsp/5ml coarsely chopped coriander root
1tsp/5ml whole black peppercorns
2tbsp/30ml light soy sauce
$^1/_2$ tsp/2.5ml sugar
4tbsp/60ml oil
8oz/240g/2 cups soft white beancurd,
each block halved lengthways, then cut diagonally
to make triangles (8 altogether)*

To garnish
*cucumber slices, onion sliced into rings
tomato segments
coriander leaves*

In a mortar pound the garlic, coriander root and peppercorns to form a paste, stir in the soy sauce and sugar. Lay the beancurd triangles in a flat dish, cover with the mixture and leave to marinate for 30 minutes.

Heat the oil and fry the marinated beancurd until golden brown. Drain and place on a serving dish garnished with cucumber, onion and tomato and decorate with coriander leaves.

*Yellow bean spicy dip on the terrace of King Mongkut's
hilltop palace*

123

MORNING GLORY IN PEANUT SAUCE

PARAM LONG SON

'Param' in the Thai title of this dish is the name of one of the heroes of the Ramayana, our national poetic epic. At one point in the story King Param takes a bath – just as the morning glory does in this recipe!

8oz/230g/1 bunch morning glory, coarsely chopped
into 2inch/5cm lengths
4oz/120g/1cup beancurd
oil for deep-frying
2tbsp/30ml oil
1tsp/5ml finely chopped garlic
1tbsp/15ml red curry paste (p. 105)
1tbsp/15ml light soy sauce
$^1/_2$tsp/2.5ml salt
1tsp/5ml sugar
4fl oz/120ml/$^1/_2$cup coconut milk
2tbsp/30ml ground roast peanuts

Bring a pan of water to the boil, blanch the morning glory for 2 minutes, drain and arrange on a serving dish. Deep-fry the beancurd until golden brown, drain, cool, then slice across the block to make long strips ¼inch/6mm thick. Arrange on top of the morning glory and set aside. Heat the 2tbsp/30ml oil and fry the garlic until golden brown. Add the red curry paste and stir briefly. Add the remaining ingredients, stirring well, bring to the boil, then pour over the prepared beancurd and morning glory and serve.

FRIED AUBERGINE WITH CHILI AND BASIL IN YELLOW BEAN SAUCE

MAKUA PAT PRIK

2tbsp/30ml oil
1tsp/5ml finely chopped garlic
3 small fresh red or green chilis, finely chopped
8oz/230g/1 large purple aubergine/eggplant, cut
into 1inch/2.5cm cubes
4tbsp/60ml vegetable stock (p. 85)
2oz/60g/$^1/_2$ sweet pepper, cut lengthways into thin
strips
1tsp/5ml yellow bean sauce
1tbsp/15ml light soy sauce
1tsp/5ml sugar
20 red basil leaves

Heat the oil and fry the garlic and chili until the garlic is golden brown. Add the aubergine, stir, add the stock and cook until the aubergine begins to soften. Add all the remaining ingredients, stirring constantly. Turn on to a serving dish.

FRIED TARO WITH CHILI SAUCE

PUAK LAAD PRIK

2tbsp/30ml plain flour
4tbsp/60ml water
¹/₂tsp/2.5ml salt
¹/₂tsp/2.5ml ground white pepper
8oz/230g/about 1 taro, peeled and sliced
1inch/2.5cm thick, then cut lengthways into 3 chips
oil for deep-frying

In a large bowl mix the flour, water, salt and pepper to form a batter. Coat the taro chips well with the batter and deep-fry until golden brown. Drain, arrange on a serving dish and set aside.

Chili Sauce
2tbsp/30ml oil
2tsp/10ml finely chopped garlic
5 small red or green chilis, finely chopped
3tbsp/45ml sugar
1tbsp/15ml tamarind juice, or 2tbsp/30ml lemon juice
4tbsp/60ml vegetable stock (p. 85)
1tsp/5ml salt
2oz/60g/¹/₂sweet pepper, finely diced

To garnish
coriander leaves

In a wok or frying pan/skillet, heat the oil and fry the garlic and chili until the garlic is golden brown. Add all the remaining ingredients, stirring constantly. Continue cooking until the sweet peppers soften, pour over the taro and garnish with coriander leaves.

STIR-FRIED CHILI AND WATER CHESTNUTS

HEL PAD PRIK HAENG

2tbsp/30ml oil
1tsp/5ml finely chopped garlic
3 large dried red chilis, coarsely sliced
3oz/90g/¹/₂cup roast cashew nuts
3oz/90g/1 small bundle long beans, chopped into
1inch/2.5cm lengths
4oz/120g/1 cup whole peeled water chestnuts
3tbsp/45ml vegetable stock (p. 85)
1tbsp/15ml light soy sauce
1tsp/5ml dark soy sauce
¹/₂tsp/2.5ml sugar

To garnish
coriander leaves

Heat the oil and fry the garlic until golden brown. Add all the ingredients in turn, stirring constantly. Turn on to a serving dish and garnish with coriander leaves.

STEAMED CURRY IN BANANA LEAF

HAW MOK Ⓔ

4×5inch/12.5cm squares banana leaf
8fl oz/240ml/1cup coconut milk
1tbsp/15ml red curry paste (p. 105)
1 egg
2tbsp/30ml light soy sauce
$^1/_2$tsp/2.5ml sugar
8oz/230g/2$^2/_3$cups oyster mushrooms, finely chopped
4oz/120g/about 8 leaves Chinese cabbage, finely chopped
20 sweet basil leaves
2 kaffir lime leaves, finely chopped
1 large fresh red chili, sliced lengthways into very thin shavings

With the banana leaves make two cups, as illustrated, and set aside (two small cups of soufflé dishes could be used instead).

In a bowl stir together the coconut milk and curry paste. Break in the egg and stir well. Add the soy sauce, sugar and mushrooms, stir well and set aside. In the bottom of the two banana cups, place the Chinese cabbage and basil leaves, and pour the prepared mixture over them. Top with kaffir lime leaf and chili. Place the cups in a hot steamer for 20 minutes. Remove and serve.

Banana Leaf Bowl

1 Place a small round bowl on a flat banana leaf. Using a sharp knife, cut around the bowl twice to create two circles of identical size (for double strength bowl).

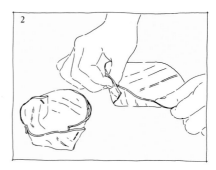

2 Putting the circles on top of each other, pinch a corner in and staple it. Repeat for each corner so that you have four stapled corners and a bowl shape.

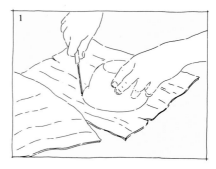

The Royal dining room in the Phra Nakhon Khiri Palace. (Back) Steamed curry and banana leaf. (Front) Stir-fried chili and water chestnuts

CRISPY NOODLES

MEE KROP Ⓔ

This complex dish is an excellent, rather sweet accompaniment to curry.

oil for deep-frying
4oz/120g dry sen mee noodles, soaked in water
for 20 minutes, and drained

The sauce
2tbsp/30ml oil
4oz/120g/1cup ready-fried beancurd, cut
into thin strips
2tbsp/30ml oil
2 garlic cloves, finely chopped
2 small shallots, finely chopped
1tbsp/15ml light soy sauce
$^1/_2$tsp/2.5ml salt
4tbsp/60ml sugar
4tsp/60ml vegetable stock (p. 85)
3tbsp/45ml lemon juice
$^1/_2$tsp/2.5ml chili powder

To garnish
2tbsp/30ml oil
1 egg, lightly beaten with 1tbsp/15ml cold water
1oz/30g/$^1/_3$cup beansprouts
1 spring onion/scallion, cut into 1inch/2.5cm slivers
1 medium-size fresh red chili, deseeded
and slivered lengthways
1 whole head pickled garlic, finely sliced across the
bulb to make flower-shaped sections

Heat the deep-frying oil until medium hot and deep-fry the drained noodles until golden brown and crisp. Drain and set aside.

Heat the oil for the sauce and fry the shredded beancurd until crisp. Remove with a slotted spoon and set aside. Add the garlic to the pan, fry until golden brown, drain and set aside. Fry the shallot until brown, add the soy sauce, salt, sugar, stock and lemon juice and stir well until the mixture begins to caramelize. Add the chili powder and the reserved beancurd and garlic and stir until they have soaked up some of the liquid. Set aside.

In a separate pan, heat the oil for the garnish and drip in the egg mixture to make little scraps of fried egg. Drain and set aside. Return the main sauce to the heat and crumble in the crispy noodles, mixing gently and briefly. Turn on to a serving dish and sprinkle with beansprouts, spring onion, fried egg scraps, chili and pickled garlic and serve.

FRIED POTATO WITH GINGER AND MUSHROOM SAUCE

MAN JIAN

8oz/230g/2–3 potatoes, sliced into rounds
$^1/_4$inch/6mm thick
oil for deep-frying
1tsp/5ml cornflour/cornstarch
2tbsp/30ml water
2tbsp/30ml oil
1tsp/5ml finely chopped garlic
2oz/60g/$^2/_3$cup pre-soaked dried
Chinese mushrooms, finely sliced
2oz/60g/1 onion, finely chopped
2inches/5cm piece ginger root, cut
into fine matchsticks
2oz/60g/$^1/_2$sweet pepper, cut lengthways into thin
strips
2 spring onions/scallions, chopped into
1inch/2.5cm lengths
4tbsp/60ml vegetable stock (p. 85)
2tbsp/30ml light soy sauce
1tsp/5ml sugar
$^1/_2$tsp/2.5ml ground white pepper

Crispy noodles

To garnish
coriander leaves

Deep-fry the potatoes until golden brown, drain, arrange on a serving dish and set aside. Mix the flour and water and set aside.

Heat the oil and fry the garlic until golden brown. Add all the ingredients in turn, stirring constantly. Finally, thicken the mixture with the flour and water. Stir well while cooking through, pour over the fried potatoes and garnish with coriander leaves.

HOT FIRE MORNING GLORY

PAK BOONG FI DAENG

This dish merits the title 'Hot Fire' because it is cooked quickly over a hot flame, and also because it is very 'chili' hot. I've struck a relatively modest position with the chilis here but you can always add more if you are feeling brave. I associate this dish with a certain noise – you always know when someone is cooking it in a market by the unmistakable loud hiss as the vegetables enter the sizzling oil.

2tbsp/30ml oil
1tsp/5ml finely chopped garlic
4 small fresh red or green chilis, finely chopped
2tsp/10ml yellow bean sauce
8oz/230g/1 bunch morning glory, coarsely chopped into 2inch/5cm lengths
4tbsp/60ml vegetable stock (p. 85)
1tbsp/15ml light soy sauce
1tsp/5ml sugar

Heat the oil and fry the garlic and chilis until the garlic is golden brown. Add the yellow beans, stir quickly, add the morning glory, stir once then add the stock and simmer until the stems of the morning glory soften slightly. Add the soy sauce and sugar, stir once then turn on to a serving dish.

FRIED BAMBOO SHOOTS WITH EGG

PAT NORMAI Ⓔ

2tbsp/30ml oil
1tsp/5ml finely chopped garlic
1 egg
8oz/230g/1 $^1/_3$ cups bamboo shoots, sliced diagonally $^1/_4$inch/6mm thick
2oz/60g/1 onion, halved then chopped into thin wedges
2 medium spring onions/scallions, finely chopped into rings
2oz/60g/$^2/_3$cup oyster mushrooms
2tbsp/30ml light soy sauce
$^1/_2$tsp/2.5ml sugar
$^1/_2$tsp/2.5ml ground white pepper

To garnish
coriander leaves

Heat the oil and fry the garlic until golden brown. Break the egg into the oil, spreading the broken yolk a little. Before the egg sets, throw in the bamboo shoots, onion, spring onion and mushrooms and stir rapidly. Add the remaining ingredients, stirring rapidly, and turn on to a serving dish.

SWEET AND SOUR VEGETABLES

PAT PREOW WAN

1tsp/5ml cornflour/cornstarch
4tbsp/60ml water
2tbsp/30ml oil
1tsp/5ml finely chopped garlic
2oz/60g/about 2 whole baby sweetcorn
2oz/60g/8–10 pineapple chunks
2oz/60g/1 small chunk cucumber, quartered then cut
into thick rings
2oz/60g/1 onion, halved, then sliced into thin
segments
2oz/60g/1 tomato, quartered
2 medium spring onions/scallions, coarsely
chopped into 1inch/2.5cm lengths
2 large fresh red chilis, sliced on the diagonal
2tbsp/30ml light soy sauce
1tsp/5ml sugar
$^1/_2$tsp/2.5ml ground white pepper

Mix the cornflour and water and set aside. Heat the oil and fry the garlic until golden brown. Add each ingredient in turn, stirring constantly. Add the flour and water mix, stirring briefly to thicken and turn on to a serving dish.

MUSHROOMS WITH GINGER

PAT KING

2tbsp/30ml oil
1tsp/5ml finely chopped garlic
2oz/60g/$^2/_3$cup pre-soaked dried black
fungus mushrooms (chop coarsely if large)
2oz/60g/1 onion, halved then chopped into thin
wedges
2oz/60g/1 carrot, cut lengthways into thin strips
2oz/60g/$^1/_2$sweet pepper, cut lengthways into thin
strips
2inches/5cm piece ginger root, cut into
fine matchsticks
2 medium spring onions/scallions, finely chopped
1tbsp/15ml light soy sauce
1tsp/5ml yellow bean sauce
$^1/_2$tsp/2.5ml sugar
4tbsp/60ml vegetable stock (p. 85)

To garnish
coriander leaves

Heat the oil and fry the garlic until golden brown. Add all the ingredients in turn, stirring constantly. Turn on to a serving dish and garnish with coriander.

MILLION YEAR EGGS

KAI PALOW Ⓔ

As readers of my first book *The Taste of Thailand* will recall, the peculiar name of this dish arose from the fact that it was one of the rare Thai meals I could make when I was a student. In consequence, I would produce it in such large quantities that my friends and I would have to eat it for days and days.

3 eggs
2tsp/10ml coarsely chopped garlic
2tsp/10ml coarsely chopped coriander root
1tsp/5ml whole black peppercorns
2tbsp/30ml oil
24fl oz/720ml/3cups vegetable stock (p. 85)
1tsp/5ml coarsely chopped ginger root
1tbsp/15ml dark soy sauce
2tbsp/30ml light soy sauce
2tbsp/30ml sugar
a pinch of salt
8oz/240g/2cups ready-fried
beancurd, cut diagonally to make 4 triangles

To garnish
coriander leaves

Hardboil the eggs, leave to cool, peel and set aside.

In a mortar, pound together the garlic, coriander root and black peppercorns to form a paste. Heat the oil in a large saucepan and briefly fry the paste. Add the vegetable stock and bring to the boil, stirring in all the ingredients down to and including the salt. Simmer briefly then add the eggs and the beancurd triangles.

Continue to simmer over a low heat for 1 hour. The eggs will have hardened and darkened. Turn into a serving bowl and garnish with coriander leaves.

FRIED VERMICELLI

PAT WUN SEN Ⓔ

2tbsp/30ml oil
1tsp/5ml finely chopped garlic
1 egg
6oz/180g vermicelli noodles, soaked and drained
2oz/60g/^{2}/$_3$cup pre-soaked dried black
fungus mushrooms, coarsely chopped
2oz/60g/1 small onion, coarsely chopped
2 spring onions/scallions, coarsely chopped
2tbsp/30ml light soy sauce
^{1}/$_2$tsp/2.5ml sugar
^{1}/$_2$tsp/2.5ml ground white pepper

To garnish
coriander leaves

Heat the oil and fry the garlic until golden brown. Break the egg into the pan, spread the yolk, and before it sets throw in the noodles, stirring quickly. Add the other ingredients in turn, stirring constantly. Turn on to a serving dish and garnish with coriander leaves.

STUFFED OMELETTE

KAI YAT SAI Ⓔ

The filling
2tbsp/30ml oil
1tsp/5ml finely chopped garlic
2oz/60g/1 onion, finely chopped
2oz/60g/$^2/_3$ cup pre-soaked dried
Chinese mushroom, finely diced
2oz/60g/$^1/_3$ cup green peas
2oz/60g/1 tomato, finely diced
1tbsp/15ml light soy sauce
$^1/_2$ tsp/2.5ml sugar
a sprinkling of ground black pepper

Heat the oil and fry the garlic until golden brown. Add all the ingredients in turn, stirring constantly. Remove from the heat and set aside.

The omelette
2 eggs
2tbsp/30ml oil

Beat the eggs. In a wok (frying pan/skillet will not do), heat the oil, turning to coat the entire inner surface. Pour in the egg and turn to spread evenly. When the egg has dried, pour the filling into the centre. Fold in the sides of the omelette to make a square 'parcel'. Cook for a moment, then lift carefully on to a dish.

In Bangkok's Weekend Market, a woman makes vegetarian stuffed omelette

HEAVENLY BEANCURD

TAO HOU SAWAN

1tbsp/15ml flour
4tbsp/60ml vegetable stock (p. 85)
2tbsp/30ml oil
1tsp/5ml finely chopped garlic
2oz/60g/¹⁄₃ cup whole straw mushrooms
4oz/120g/2 medium broccoli stems, sliced diagonally
¹⁄₄inch/6mm thick
2oz/60g/1 carrot, finely sliced
1tbsp/15ml light soy sauce
1tsp/5ml dark soy sauce
¹⁄₂tsp/2.5ml sugar
¹⁄₂tsp/2.5ml ground white pepper
8oz/240g/2cups soft white beancurd, quartered

Mix the flour and stock and set aside.

Heat the oil, fry the garlic golden brown then add the remaining ingredients in turn, stirring constantly. Add the beancurd and stir well. Mix in the flour and stock and stir to thicken. Turn on to a serving dish and to impress arrange as shown in the photograph.

MUSHROOMS IN RED SAUCE

HET HOM NAM DAENG

2tbsp/30ml oil
1tsp/5ml finely chopped garlic
6oz/180g/2cups pre-soaked dried
Chinese mushrooms
4oz/120g/2 medium broccoli stems, cut into florets
1tbsp/15ml light soy sauce
1tsp/5ml dark soy sauce
4tbsp/60ml vegetable stock (p. 85)
2oz/60g/1 tomato, finely diced
1tsp/5ml flour
1inch/2.5cm piece ginger root, cut into fine
matchsticks
¹⁄₂tsp/2.5ml chili powder

Heat the oil and fry the garlic golden brown. Cut the mushrooms in half if large, add to the garlic with the broccoli and briefly stir-fry. Add both soy sauces, stir, add the stock and tomato, stir, add the flour and stir to thicken a little. Add the ginger and chili powder, stirring well. Turn on to a serving dish and arrange decoratively.

(Left) Heavenly beancurd; (right) mushrooms in red sauce

LEMON GRASS SPICY VEGETABLES

PAT PET TAKRAI

This is another delicious creation from my friends at The Lemon Grass restaurant in Bangkok. As you can tell from the long list of ingredients it is full of fascinating flavours and textures and is well worth the effort involved in cutting and slicing before you start cooking.

2 large dried red chilis, coarsely chopped
1tsp/5ml coarsely chopped galangal
2 small red shallots, coarsely chopped
3oz/90g/^{3}/$_4$cup ready-fried beancurd
finely diced
oil for deep-frying
2tbsp/30ml oil
1tsp/5ml finely chopped garlic
1tbsp/15ml lemon grass, finely chopped into rings
1tbsp/15ml grated coconut
2oz/60g/1 small bundle long beans, coarsely
chopped into 1inch/2.5cm lengths
2oz/60g/1 medium broccoli stem, coarsely chopped
at an angle into 1inch/2.5cm lengths
2oz/60g/about 4 baby sweetcorn, roughly chopped
at an angle into 1inch/2.5cm lengths
2oz/60g/1 carrot, finely chopped into matchsticks
3tbsp/45ml vegetable stock (p. 85)
2tbsp/30ml light soy sauce
^{1}/$_2$tsp/2.5ml sugar

In a mortar, pound together the chilis, galangal and shallots to form a paste and set aside. Deep-fry the beancurd dice until crispy brown, drain and set aside.

Heat the 2tbsp/30ml oil and fry the garlic golden brown. Stir in the paste, add the lemon grass and coconut, stirring well. Add all the vegetables and briefly stir-fry. Add the stock, soy sauce and sugar. Stir well and turn on to a serving dish.

FRIED BEANCURD WITH BASIL LEAF

TAO HOU PAT KRAPOW

oil for deep-frying
8oz/240g/2cups soft white beancurd halved
to make 4 pieces
2tbsp/30ml oil
1tsp/5ml finely chopped garlic
4 small red or green chilis, finely chopped
2oz/60g/^{2}/$_3$cup straw mushrooms, halved
2oz/60g/1 small bundle long beans, finely diced into
rings
1oz/30g/^{1}/$_2$small sweet pepper, finely sliced
lengthways into slivers
2tbsp/30ml light soy sauce
^{1}/$_2$tsp/2.5ml sugar
20 red basil leaves

Deep-fry the beancurd until golden brown, drain and set aside. Heat the 2tbsp/30ml oil and fry the garlic and chilis until the garlic is golden brown. Add the deep-fried beancurd, breaking it up in the pan as you stir-fry. Add all the remaining ingredients in turn, stirring constantly. Turn on to a serving dish.

Lemon grass spicy vegetables – a speciality of the Lemon Grass Restaurant in Bangkok

FRIED BEANCURD WITH VEGETABLES IN YELLOW BEAN SAUCE

TAO HOU LAHD NAA

8oz/240g/2 cups soft white beancurd quartered to
make 8 cubes
sufficient fine breadcrumbs to coat the beancurd
oil for deep-frying
1tsp/5ml cornflour/cornstarch mixed with a little
water to make a thin paste
2tbsp/30ml oil
1tsp/5ml finely chopped garlic
2oz/60g/about 10 mangetout/snow peas, topped and
tailed
2oz/60g/1 medium broccoli stem, cut into florets
2oz/60g/¹/₂ sweet red pepper, cut lengthways into
slivers
2oz/60g/about 4 baby sweetcorn, finely sliced
4tbsp/60ml vegetable stock (p. 85)
1tsp/5ml yellow bean sauce
1tbsp/15ml light soy sauce
¹/₂tsp/2.5ml sugar
¹/₂tsp/2.5ml ground white pepper

Coat the beancurd with breadcrumbs and deep-fry until golden brown. Drain, arrange on a serving dish and set aside. Heat the 2tbsp/30ml oil and fry the garlic golden brown. Add the vegetables in turn, constantly stirring. Pour in the vegetable stock and stir well, add the yellow beans, soy sauce, sugar and pepper, stirring well, then add the flour and water paste, stirring briefly to thicken. Pour over the beancurd and serve.

SPICY BEANCURD

CHU CHEE TAO HOU

8oz/240g/2cups soft white beancurd
cut into ¹/₂inch/1.25cm squares
oil for deep-frying
2tbsp/30ml oil
1tbsp/15ml red curry paste (p. 105)
2tbsp/30ml light soy sauce
2tbsp/30ml sugar
4tbsp/60ml vegetable stock (p. 85)
2tbsp/30ml ground roast peanuts
2 small red chilis, finely chopped
2 kaffir lime leaves, rolled into cigarettes then finely
slivered

Deep-fry the beancurd squares until golden brown, drain and arrange on a serving dish and set aside. Heat the 2tbsp/30ml oil and briefly fry the curry paste, add the soy sauce, sugar and vegetable stock, mixing well. Add the ground peanuts, chilis and kaffir lime leaf slivers. Reduce the heat and simmer until the sugar thickens the sauce. Pour over the deep-fried beancurd and serve.

NAM PRIK

One dish unites the whole of Thailand – north and south, rich and poor – Nam Prik. Literally 'chili water', Nam Prik is a thickened, heavily spiced liquid used either as a piquant sauce or as a rich dip served with crudités, salads or blanched vegetables. In many parts of the country Nam Prik with rice and a few vegetables and river fish is the staple diet of farming communities – and very tasty and healthy it is. Transformed in the grand kitchens of the city, Nam Prik becomes a flamboyant presentation piece with bouquets of carved vegetables and sprays of multi-coloured salads ranged around the bowl of sauce.

For vegetarians, Nam Prik is the perfect dinner party dish, substantial yet pleasing to look at. You can let your imagination run riot over the choice and presentation of the accompaniments – almost anything will do, from deep-fried potato crisps/chips to raw cucumber.

GREEN MANGO NAM PRIK

NAM PRIK MAMUANG

2tsp/10ml coarsely chopped garlic
6 small red or green chilis, coarsely chopped
4oz/120g/about 1 young sour green mango,
peeled, cut
from the stone and
coarsely chopped
1tbsp/15ml light soy sauce
1tbsp/15ml lemon juice
1tbsp/15ml sugar

In a mortar, pound together the garlic and chili. Add the mango and lightly pound to soften, turning with a spoon. When roughly broken and mixed add the soy sauce, lemon juice and sugar and mix well. Turn into a bowl and serve with salads, crudités or blanched vegetables.

NORTHERN NAM PRIK

NAM PRIK NUM

2 large fresh young green chilis
4 small fresh red or green chilis
2 large garlic cloves, peeled
2 small shallots, peeled
1 medium tomato
1 round green aubergine/eggplant (p. 56)
2tbsp/30ml lemon juice
2tbsp/30ml light soy sauce
1/2tsp/2.5ml salt
1tsp/5ml sugar

Wrap the first 6 ingredients in foil and place under a grill/broiler until they begin to soften. Remove from the heat, place in a mortar and pound together to form a soft liquid paste. Add the remaining ingredients to the paste in turn, stirring well.

Turn into a bowl and serve with a selection of salads or fresh or blanched vegetables. Deep-fried battered mushrooms are especially good.

CHINESE CELERY WITH CHILIS IN OIL

NAM PRIK POW PAT KUNCHAI

The Thai word 'pow' means grilled/broiled and in the past the ingredients were lightly charred on an open fire. As this would be difficult today I have adapted the dish for the modern kitchen – you could however capture something of the original on a garden barbecue.

Leave the seeds in the chili if you want the sauce very hot. If you can't get Chinese celery, ordinary celery will suffice.

Chilis In Oil (Nam Prik Pow)
4tbsp/60ml oil
3tbsp/45ml finely chopped garlic
3tbsp/45ml finely chopped shallots
3 large dry red chilis, deseeded and coarsely chopped
2tbsp/30ml sugar
1tsp/5ml salt

Heat the oil, fry the garlic until golden brown, remove with a slotted spoon and set aside. In the same oil fry the shallots until crispy, remove and set aside. Fry the chilis until they darken, remove and place in a mortar with the shallot and garlic. Pound together. Reheat the oil, add the paste and warm through. Add the sugar and salt and mix well to give a thick black/red sauce.

The vegetables
2tbsp/30ml oil
1tsp/5ml finely chopped garlic
1tbsp/15ml chilis in oil, nam prik pow (above)
4oz/120g/1 1/3 cups pre-soaked dried Chinese mushrooms, coarsely chopped
6oz/180g/3 stalks Chinese celery, coarsely chopped into 1 1/2 inch/4cm lengths
2tbsp/30ml light soy sauce
1/2tsp/2.5ml sugar
2tbsp/30ml vegetable stock (p. 85)

Heat the oil and fry the garlic golden brown. Quickly stir in the prepared sauce, add the mushrooms and celery and stir well. Add the remaining ingredients, stirring well. Turn on to a serving dish.

Northern **Nam Prik** *by a ruined temple*

DESSERTS

THE PETCHABURI ROAD

On the road that leads into Petchaburi from Bang-kok, the traveller passes what at first glance appears to be the usual cluster of roadside restaurants. In a way they are just that: they offer perfectly straight-forward meals, but that is not why so many people pull off the road and visit them. The attraction is the multi-coloured array of sweets and desserts on sale. Petch-aburi is the sweet-tooth capital of Thailand and no-one passing can resist sampling one or two delicacies and then buying in a few more to take home as presents.

The reason we like to buy Thai sweets is because most of them are difficult to make at home and are usually only prepared on special occasions. A normal Thai meal ends with fruit, and as Thai tropical fruits are among the world's most succulent this is no hardship. Thai mangosteens and rambutans are increasingly marketed throughout the world and I imagine that you will choose to settle for fruit as your main dessert course. Just occasionally Thai shops in the West do offer one or two cooked desserts, usually made by a member of the local Thai community, but if you really want to experience Thai sweets you will have to make the effort yourself. There will be no surer way to

(Left to right) Rambutan; guava and rose apple; mangosteen; lychee

143

Grilling bananas

impress dinner party guests for Thai sweets are wonderful to look at as well as delightful to eat.

Thai desserts normally fall into one of two categories. Liquid desserts consist of fruits and vegetables served in coconut milk or sugar syrup; and solid desserts take the form of little cakes or jellies. Taste is crucial; sweet and rich are often balanced with a touch of saltiness, but just as important are appearance and fragrance. Much effort goes into moulding outlines and creating subtle liquid colours to ensure that a dessert is visually appealing. Such labour finds its apogee in Look Choob, miniature vegetables moulded out of sweet bean paste and glazed with vibrant colours. Few can make Look Choob and it is seldom served other than on very special occasions.

The commonest way of perfuming a dessert is to include flowers such as jasmine in the recipe; more unusual is the practice of placing tiny cakes (kanom) in an earthenware pot with a little cup of burning incense which will suffuse them with its aroma. The art of perfuming sweetmeats is as tricky as making Look Choob; too much incense or too many fresh flowers in a dish results in a bad smell!

I am not recommending that you should experiment with such rarified activities at home: just as the creation of French patisserie is best left to experts, so with the advanced forms of Thai dessert-making, but we can all try our hands at an authentic homemade pudding.

PUMPKIN IN COCONUT CREAM

GAENG BUAD FAK TONG

8fl oz/240g/1 cup coconut milk
8oz/230g/^{1}/$_2$ small pumpkin, peeled and cut into
1inch/2.5cm squares
^{1}/$_2$ inch/1.25cm thick
2tbsp/30ml sugar
a pinch of salt

In a pan, bring the coconut milk to the boil, add the pumpkin, sugar and salt and simmer briefly until the pumpkin is soft. Turn into a serving dish.

DURIAN WITH COCONUT SWEET STICKY RICE

NAM GRATI DURIAN

The durian is South East Asia's most notorious fruit – the experience of eating it was once described as being something like consuming a crème caramel over an open sewer. It looks like an American football with spikes on it and when a section of this hard outer shell is hacked away the soft yellow fruit can be seen inside. Unfortunately this also releases a smell which so revolts Western sensibilities that most airlines forbid passengers to carry them on board. This used to result in an annual stampede of European durian lovers heading East, flying out when the fruit was in season, for despite the smell many became totally addicted to the rich yellow flesh.

Today, some airlines will transport the fruit as cargo and you can even find segments of durian on the cool shelves of oriental supermarkets. These ready prepared segments have far less odour than that given off when the shell is broken open. All this has made the durian far more accessible. If you are simply eating the raw fruit it is useful to know that connoisseurs prefer it slightly firm. When it softens it is better used in prepared dishes such as this one.

Coconut sweet sticky rice
4fl oz/120ml/^{1}/$_2$ cup coconut milk
^{1}/$_2$ tsp/2.5ml salt
2oz/60g/^{1}/$_4$ cup sugar
8oz/230g/2 cups freshly cooked sticky rice (p. 50)
(still warm)
2tbsp/30ml oil

In a bowl mix the coconut milk, salt and sugar until the latter has dissolved. Stir in the still warm sticky rice and the oil and set aside.

The durian
8fl oz/240ml/1 cup coconut milk
3oz/90g/^{1}/$_3$ cup sugar
^{1}/$_2$ tsp/2.5ml salt
10oz/300g/about 1 ripe durian fruit, de-stoned/pitted

Heat the coconut milk, salt and sugar until the latter dissolves. Remove from the heat and allow to cool. Place the durian pieces in the cooled mixture and briefly soak. Arrange the durian on a serving dish beside the sweet sticky rice.

CRISP RUBIES

Tap tim grob

This dish is incredibly finicky to make, but it is wonderfully delicate and colourful and just the thing to eat out of doors on a summer's day.

4oz/120g/1 cup water chestnuts, diced into
¹/₄inch/6mm cubes
pink food dye
4oz/120g/1cup flour
8oz/230g/1cup sugar
8fl oz/240ml/1cup water
2 bandan leaves
8fl oz/240ml/1cup coconut milk
crushed ice

Pour the pink food colour into a shallow bowl and dip one corner of each water chestnut cube into the dye so that half of it is reddish pink (they should look like pomegranate seeds). This is difficult and time-consuming, but gives the dish its undoubted appeal. Spread the flour on a plate and gently roll each dipped cube until it is lightly coated.

Bring a pan of water to the boil and plunge in the cubes. When they rise to the surface, remove and plunge into cold water to arrest the cooking, drain and set aside.

Boil the sugar and water to make a syrup, add one bandan leaf and simmer until the syrup begins to thicken. Set aside.

Bring the coconut milk and remaining bandan leaf to the boil, stirring well. Remove from the heat.

Divide the water chestnut cubes between 4 individual serving bowls. Add the syrup and stir to separate the cubes. Pour the coconut milk over the cubes, add a little crushed ice and serve. The bandan leaves are left in, but are not eaten.

On the summit of the Maha Sawan, or 'Great Heaven' – (front) pumpkin in coconut cream; (middle) crisp rubies; (top) durian with coconut cream and sticky rice; (back) durian

LOTUS SEEDS IN COCONUT MILK

BUA LOY LOOK BUA

Although the ingredients for this recipe may seem unusual, any large oriental store should have them and the dish is surprisingly easy to make. Its main attraction, however, is that it can be made in large quantities with little effort and is often produced for festivals and village fêtes in Thailand. It would be the perfect sweet for a party of any kind.

8oz/230g/2 cups glutinous rice flour
4fl oz/120ml/¹/₂ cup water
2fl oz/60ml/¹/₄ cup bandan leaf juice (p. 152)
1oz/30g/¹/₄ cup tapioca flour
16floz/480ml/2 cups coconut milk
4oz/120g/¹/₂ cup sugar
8fl oz/240g/1 cup water
¹/₂ tsp/2.5ml salt
6oz/180g/1 cup tinned lotus seeds, drained

Place the first 4 ingredients in a large bowl and knead to a thick dough. Form the dough into small balls, roughly the size of the lotus seeds and place in a pan of boiling water until they are cooked, when they will rise to the surface. Drain and set aside.

In a large pan heat the coconut milk, sugar, water and salt, stirring well until a thick soup is produced. Add the lotus seeds, stir, add the cooked dough balls, stir well, turn into small bowls and serve.

MANGO WITH STICKY RICE

KHAONEOW MAMUANG

This is Thailand's most famous dessert, the one preferred by visitors. We often eat it on its own as an afternoon snack. Once you have mastered the art of sweet sticky rice, this is simplicity itself.

1 batch sweet sticky rice (p. 152)
3 large ripe mangoes
2tbsp/30ml coconut cream

Peel the mango and cut it lengthways into two 'cheeks' by slicing as close to the stone as possible. There's usually quite a bit of flesh left around the stone, so the cook gets that as a reward! Slice each cheek into four, crossways, and arrange on a serving dish beside the sweet sticky rice. Pour the coconut cream over the rice and serve.

Mango and sticky rice

STEAMED CUSTARD IN COCONUT

SANGKAYA MAPROW ON Ⓔ

You will need two young green coconuts. Cut them as illustrated, to make a roughly conical container. You may drink the coconut juice (refreshing when chilled) but should leave the soft flesh.

1 Take a young green coconut and pare off the sides to make a diamond shape, with a flat base. This conical container contains the actual coconut, the meat and the milk.

2 Cut the top of the diamond shape and pour off the milk. Add the custard to hollow cavity, on top of the meat. Replace the lid and put the whole thing into a steamer and steam for 25 minutes.

16fl oz/480ml/2 cups coconut milk
8oz/230g/1 cup sugar
6 egg whites (you could use the yolks to make
Foy Tong, p. 151)

Place the ingredients in a bowl and whisk together. Pour into the coconut containers and cover with the 'lids'. Place in a steamer over boiling water for 25–30 minutes. You can test whether the custard is cooked by lifting the caps and inserting a skewer into the centre of the custard. If the skewer comes out cleanly the dish is ready. Serve with a spoon to scoop out the custard.

MOONG BEANS IN COCONUT MILK

TOW SUAN

The idea of beans being transformed into a dessert may not seem immediately appealing to Western tastes. But in fact the mix of sour and sweet in this dish exactly conforms to the oriental ideal of balance and is well worth the effort in overcoming any prejudices.

4oz/120g/^{2}/$_3$cup dried moong beans, soaked in
water for 20 minutes
24fl oz/620ml/2^1/$_2$cups water
8oz/230g/1cup sugar
4oz/120g/1cup flour
4fl oz/120ml/^{1}/$_2$cup coconut milk
^{1}/$_2$tsp/2.5ml salt

Strain the moong beans, place in boiling water and cook until swollen. Add the sugar and flour (it is advisable to mix a little cold water with the flour beforehand so that it will mix smoothly). Stir well until the mixture thickens and pour into serving dishes. Warm the coconut milk and salt and pour a little over each bowl to taste.

GOLD THREADS

FOY TONG Ⓔ

The use of eggs in Thai desserts is said to have begun with the arrival of the Portuguese in the sixteenth century. This led to the use of flowers so as to disguise the 'egginess' with perfume.

Making gold threads

The process of making the threads for this dish is a little complicated, but fortunately we were able to photograph it on the eve of a fête at a village temple. You will need to make a special piece of equipment – clean an empty tin can and pierce the base with six small holes through which liquid can be streamed.

10 jasmine flowers
16fl oz/480ml/2cups water
10 eggs
1tsp/5ml oil
2lb/900g/4cups sugar

Place the jasmine flowers in the water to perfume it and set aside.

Separate the yolks and reserve 2tbsp/30ml clear egg white. Whisk the yolks, add the reserved egg white and the oil and whisk again. Remove the jasmine flowers, pour the perfumed water into a large pan with the sugar and heat to a bubbling thin syrup. Take the tin can strainer and moving in a circle over the syrup, dribble in thin streams of egg mixture to form loose 'nests' of threads. Cook for one minute, remove with a stick or skewer and place on a metal tray to cool.

COCONUT CLUSTERS

MAPROW GEOW

1 ¹/₂lb/680g/3cups sugar
12fl oz/360ml/1 ¹/₂cups water
8oz/230g/1cup coconut slivers (use a cheese grater)

In a pan, heat the sugar and water to make a thick syrup. Remove from the heat. With the fingers, make a loose ball of coconut, dip in the syrup, remove and place on a metal tray to harden.

BANANAS IN THICK SYRUP

KRUAY CHU'AM

8oz/230g/1cup sugar
8fl oz/240ml/1cup water
4 large bananas
4fl oz/120ml/$^1/_2$cup coconut milk
$^1/_4$tsp/1.25ml salt

In a small saucepan, dissolve the sugar in the water. Strain through muslin/cheesecloth into a larger pan. Peel the bananas and chop into 2inch/5cm pieces. Add to the sugar mixture and boil. Lower the heat and cook gently, removing any scum that forms, until the bananas are bright and clear and the sugar syrup forms threads when lifted with a wooden spoon. Serve hot as is or with the coconut milk mixed with salt to balance the sweetness.

SWEET STICKY RICE

KHAONEOW GEOW

This simple recipe is as decorative as it is tasty and you will probably want to use it in combination with some other sweet or fruit. You can run riot with the food dyes and making it can be a lot of fun for children.

8oz/230g/2cups cooked sticky rice (p. 50)
1 $^1/_2$lb/680g/3cups sugar
12fl oz/360ml/1 $^1/_2$ cups water
Food dyes, optional

Divide up the rice and dip it in different food dyes as fancy dictates. Heat the sugar and water to form a thick syrup and remove from the heat. With fingers, form the coloured rice into balls and dip in the syrup. Remove and place on a metal tray to harden.

WATER CHESTNUTS WITH BANDAN LEAF AND COCONUT CREAM

TAKO HEL

Bandan leaf can now be found outside of Asia. You will need to buy an entire cut plant with about 10 leaves. The leaves should be pounded in a mortar to give 4fl oz/ 120ml/ $^1/_2$ cup juice.

24fl oz/720ml/3cups water
10 jasmine flowers
8oz/230g/2cups rice flour
4fl oz/120ml/ $^1/_2$cup bandan leaf juice (see above)
8oz/230g/2cups water chestnuts, finely diced
8oz/230g/1 cup sugar

Place the jasmine flowers in the water for an hour to perfume it.

Remove the jasmine from the water. In a large pan, heat the water and add the rice flour, bandan juice, water chestnuts and sugar, stirring constantly until the mixture thickens. Turn into small serving bowls and set aside.

The coconut cream
2oz/60g/ $^1/_2$cup rice flour
8fl oz/240ml/1 cup coconut cream
$^1/_4$tsp/1.25ml salt

In a saucepan gently heat all the ingredients until the mixture thickens. Pour a little over each bowl and serve.

In Bangkok's flower market, a selection of sweets: (top and bottom) bananas in thick syrup; (centre) sweet sticky rice; (left) water chestnuts with bandan leaf; (right) coconut clusters

Golden egg drops

Place the jasmine flowers in the water to perfume it and set aside. If you cannot find jasmine, substitute a few drops of flower water, such as rose water.

Separate the egg yolks, reserving 2tbsp/30ml clear egg white. Whisk together the egg yolks, the reserved white, and the flour. Set aside.

Remove the jasmine flowers and heat the water with the sugar to make a gently simmering syrup. Drop a teaspoon of the egg mixture into the syrup so that a tear-shaped ball is formed. Cook for one minute. Remove with a strainer or slotted spoon and place on a metal tray to cool. Repeat until all the mixture is used.

BANANAS IN COCONUT MILK

KLUAY BUAD CHEE

4 large bananas
12fl oz/375ml/1 1/2 cups coconut milk
2tbsp/30ml sugar
1/2 tsp/2.5ml salt

Peel the bananas then chop into 2inch/5cm segments. Heat the coconut milk with the sugar and salt until the sugar dissolves. Add the banana pieces and cook gently for 5 minutes.

Divide between 4–6 bowls and serve warm.

GOLDEN EGG DROPS

TONG YOD Ⓔ

16fl oz/480ml/2cups water
10 jasmine flowers
10 eggs
2tbsp/15ml flour
1lb/450g sugar

BANANA FRITTERS

KANOM FAK BUA Ⓔ

Because the Thai name means 'Blossoming Lotus Flower' this dish is thought to symbolize happiness and prosperity and is thus very popular at wedding feasts. You'll see how the name came about as you watch the mixture 'blossom' in the hot oil.

8oz/230g/2cups flour
4fl oz/120ml/$^1/_2$cup water
1 medium banana, mashed to a pulp
1 egg
6tbsp/90ml sugar
oil for deep-frying

In a bowl, mix all the ingredients except the oil together to make a thick soup. Heat the oil until gently simmering and carefully pour into it a tablespoonful of the mixture so that it 'blossoms' into a round patty. Cook until golden brown, drain and set aside. Repeat until all the mixture is used.

LONGAN WITH STICKY RICE AND COCONUT CREAM

KHAONEOW PEEAK LAMYAI

The longan is similar to a lychee. Some oriental stores call them 'dragon's eyes'.

4oz/125g/1cup uncooked sticky rice (p. 50)
48fl oz/1.5l/6 cups water
7oz/210g/1cup sugar
8oz/230g/2cups longans, de-stoned/pitted
8fl oz/240ml/1cup coconut milk
$^1/_2$tsp/2.5ml salt

Wash the rice, drain then cook in the water for 15–20 minutes until the rice swells and a thick soup is produced. Add the sugar and stir until dissolved. Add the longans and stir briefly then pour into small bowls. Mix the coconut milk and salt and pour a little over each bowl to taste.

Sago and sweetcorn in coconut milk

SAGO AND SWEETCORN IN COCONUT MILK

SA KU KOW POD

4fl oz/120ml/$^1/_2$cup coconut milk
$^1/_2$tsp/2.5ml salt
64fl oz/1.9l/8cups water
2oz/60g/$^1/_3$cup uncooked sago (p. 14)
8oz/230g/1cup sugar
4oz/120g/1cup ready-cooked sweetcorn off the cob

Dissolve the salt in the coconut milk. Cook the sago in boiling water until it swells, add the sugar and sweetcorn and cook briefly. Turn into serving bowls and cover with coconut and salt mixture to taste.

MENU PLANNER

The following are five suggested menus for a balanced meal for four people. I have chosen those dishes with the easiest to find ingredients but you can alter the composition at will and should always feel free to make new combinations of recipes from time to time.

MENU ONE

Salad of black fungus mushrooms – Yam het hoo noo (p. 47)
Deep fried yellow bean paste – Baa yir (p. 72)
Rice
White beancurd soup – Gaeng jud tao hou kow (p. 97)
Green curry with aubergine and coconut – Gaeng keow wan (p. 113)
Spicy quick-fried long beans – Pat prik king (p. 113)
Yellow bean spicy dip with crudités – Tow jeow lon (p. 123)
Banana in coconut milk – Kluay buad chee (p. 154)

MENU TWO

Green papaya salad – Som tam (p. 53)
Mushroom satay – Satay het hom (p. 66)
Rice
Cauliflower, coconut and galangal soup – Tom ka (p. 97)
Mixed vegetable curry – Gaeng ped pak (p. 106)
Fried beancurd with basil leaf – Tao hou pat krapow (p. 136)
Green mango nam prik – Nam prik mamuang (p. 139)
Sago and sweet corn in coconut milk – Sa ku kow pod (p. 155)

MENU THREE

Spicy mixed vegetable salad – Yam pak ruam mit (p. 51)
Vegetable samosas – Sa mo sa (p. 76)
Rice
Hot and sour mushroom soup – Tom yam het (p. 87)
Chiang Mai curry – Gaeng haeng lay (p. 108)
Fried aubergine/eggplant with chili and basil leaf in yellow bean sauce – Makua pat prik (p. 124)
Fried potato with ginger and mushroom sauce – Man jian (p. 128)
Crisp Rubies – Tap tim grob (p. 147)

MENU FOUR

Oyster mushroom yam – Yam pow hoo (p. 47)
Fried beancurd with sweet nut sauce – Tao hou tod (p. 67)
Rice
Sago soup – Gaeng jud sa ku (p. 88)
Pineapple curry – Gaeng kua sapparot (p. 112)
Mushroom with ginger – Pat king (p. 131)
Steamed curry in banana leaf – Haw mok (p. 126)
Lotus seeds in coconut milk – Bua loy look bua (p. 148)

MENU FIVE

Beancurd salad – Yam tao hou (p. 57)
Sweetcorn cakes – Tod man khao pohd (p. 79)
Rice
Vermicelli soup – Gaeng wun sen (p. 92)
Massaman curry – Gaeng massaman (p. 114)
Stir fried chili and waterchestnuts – Hel pad prik haeng (p. 125)
Northern nam prik – Nam prik num (p. 140)
Mango with sticky rice – Khaoneow mamuang (p. 148)

USEFUL ADDRESSES

Most restaurants in Thailand will make a meat-free meal on request and there is usually a number of vegetable dishes on every menu. But you should be aware that unless you specifically request otherwise these dishes will be prepared with fish sauce, nam pla, the basic condiment of Thailand. If this is unacceptable you must ask them to substitute light soy sauce for fish sauce.

The following restaurants serve Thai vegetarian food:

The Whole Earth
93/3 Soi Lang Suan, Ploenchit Rd, Bangkok. Tel: 2525574
This is the only true vegetarian restaurant in the capital apart from the vegetarian pavilion at the Weekend Market. There is a sister restaurant in the northern capital of Chiang Mai.

The Whole Earth, Chiang Mai
88 Sridonchai Rd, Chiang Mai. Tel: 232463

Lemongrass
5/1 Sukhumvit 24, Bangkok. Tel: 2588637
This is Thai haute cuisine at its best with vegetarian dishes on request, in a charming setting of antiques, old and modern paintings and bric-à-brac.

Ban Krua
29/1 Saladaeng Soi 1, Bangkok. Tel: 2336912
A short walk from the main business district around Silom Rd, the Ban Krua is small but friendly. You can eat outside or in an airconditioned room.

Seven Seas
14/7 Sukhumvit 33, Bangkok. Tel: 2597662
One of the capital's currently fashionable restaurants run by a young nobleman, Mom Luang Chirathorn, whose knowledge of fine cooking extends to the vegetarian dishes that will be made on request.

Once Upon A Time
167 Soi Anumanrachaton, Bangkok. Tel: 2338493
Situated between Surawong Rd and Silom Rd, this restaurant is a true find as it occupies one of the few remaining wooden 'colonial' houses in the centre of town and is now entirely surrounded by towering office blocks. Go for the nostalgic decoration as well as for the excellent food.

Tumnak Thai
Ruchadapisek Rd, Bangkok. Tel: 2761810
According to *The Guinness Book of Records* this is the biggest restaurant in the world, though in a sense it is a complex of different restaurants, each in its own style of Thai architecture and each specializing in the food of one of the country's different regions. There is ample vegetarian food.

Kuk Kak Rest-Area
20/1 MU4 Bangpakong, Banga-Trad Rd, Chachiengsao. Tel: 038 531856
This is a real curiosity, a vegetarian wayside inn on the route between Bangkok and the seaside resort of Pattaya. As well as food, the rest-area offers a moment's repose in the country, with views over the rice fields and seats outside.

HOTELS

The following hotels serve vegetarian meals.

The Tara Hotel
183/1 Sukhumvit Soi 26, Bangkok. Tel: 2592900
In reality this is two hotels linked together, the sister hotel being the slightly cheaper Impala. The Impala's excellent lunchtime buffet has a vegetarian section.

The Dusit Thani Hotel
Rama IV Rd, Bangkok. Tel: 2361450/9
The Dusit Thani remains one of Thailand's best hotels. The Pavilion Café has a number of vegetarian dishes on offer.

The Regent Hotel
155 Rajadamri Rd, Bangkok. Tel: 2516532
This is in the de luxe category but even if you aren't staying there you should visit The Spice Market restaurant to see the wonderful wooden decoration that recreates the authentic look of an old spice store. The food is delicious and, not surprisingly, spicy.

The Ambassador Hotel
171 Sukhumvit Soi II. Bangkok. Tel. 2515141
This hotel contains a food complex with sections for Thai, Chinese, Japanese and Western food. Among them is a Thai vegetarian café and a superb Chinese vegetarian restaurant.

INDEX OF RECIPES

159